Netherlandic Secular Plays from the Middle Ages

The "Abele Spelen" and the Farces of the Hulthem Manuscript

Carleton Renaissance Plays in Translation **29**

General Editors
Donald Beecher, Douglas Campbell, Massimo Ciavolella

The last page of *Esmoreit* and the beginning of *Lippijn*, from the Hulthem Manuscript.

Carleton Renaissance Plays in Translation

Netherlandic Secular Plays from the Middle Ages

The "Abele Spelen" and the Farces of the Hulthem Manuscript

Translated with

an Introduction and Notes

by

Theresia de Vroom

Dovehouse Editions Inc.
Ottawa, Canada
1997

Acknowledgments

This book is published with the financial assistance of The Administratie Kunst, Muziek, Letteren, Podiumkunst, Ministerie van de Vlaamse Gemeenschap, Brussels, for which the publishers express their gratitude.

Canadian Cataloguing in Publication Data
Main entry under title:
Netherlandic secular plays from the Middle Ages: the Abele Spelen and farces of the Hulthem Manuscript.

(Carleton Renaissance plays in translation ; 29)
Includes bibliographical references.

ISBN 1-895537-41-X (bound) .–
ISBN 1-895537-35-5 (pbk.)

1. Dutch drama — Translation into English. I. Vroom, Theresia de. II. Series.

PT5445.E5N48 1997   839.3'12108   C96-901017-6

Copyright © 1997 Dovehouse Editions, Canada

For information and orders write to:
> Dovehouse Editions
> 1890 Fairmeadow Cres.
> Ottawa, Canada, K1H 7B9

For information on the series:
> Carleton Renaissance Plays in Translation
> c/o Department of English
> Carleton University
> 1125 Colonel By Drive
> Ottawa, Canada K1S 5B6

No part of this book may be translated or reproduced in any form, by print, microfilm, photoprint, or any other means, without written permission from the publisher.

Typeset in Canada: Carleton Production Centre
Manufactured in Canada

Cover illustration: "Sanderijn meets the Knight," printed by Willem Vosterman, Antwerp ca. 1518. Bayerische Staatsbibliothek, Munich Rar. 990.

For Robert W. Hellwarth

Want ic nie man op eerde en sach,
Dien ic meer doeghden an
Dan ic doe minen lieven man.
Hets recht, want hi eest wel weert:
Hi es een ridder wide vermeert....

Lanseloet v. 769–773

Table of Contents

List of Illustrations	8
Acknowledgments	9
Introduction	11
Bibliography	59
Netherlandic Secular Plays:	
The "Abele Spelen" and the	
Farces of the Hulthem Manuscript	65
Esmoreit	67
Lippijn	101
Gloriant	109
The Box-Blower	147
Lanseloet of Denmark	155
The Witch	189
Of the Winter and of the Summer	195
Rubben	217
Truwanten	227
Three Days Lord	233

List of Illustrations

1. The last page of *Esmoreit* and the beginning of *Lippijn*, from the Hulthem Manuscript. — 2
2. Detail from the *Allegory of Temperance*, by P. Bruegel, "a morality play." Rotterdam, Museum Boymans-van Beuningen. — 10
3. P. Bruegel, *The Calumny of Apelles*. London, British Museum. — 66
4. Dissimulation: "carrying both fire and water," by P. Bruegel, from *Netherlandish Proverbs* or *The Blue Cloak*. Berlin-Dahlem, Staatliche Museen. — 100
5. Flemish tapestry, "A Noble Company," documenting the influence of Islamic and Oriental elements in the fashions of the Middle Ages. The Cloisters, New York. — 108
6. P. Bruegel, "Two Peasants." Cleveland Museum of Art. — 146
7. "Lanseloet courts Sanderijn," *Lanseloet van Denemarken*. Gouda: Govert van Ghemen, ca. 1486–92. — 154
8. "Lanseloet's mother tricks Sanderijn," *Lanseloet van Denemarken*. Gouda: Govert van Ghemen, ca. 1486–92. — 165
9. "Sanderijn meets the Knight," *Lanseloet van Denemarken*. Gouda: Govert van Ghemen, ca. 1486–92. — 169
10. "The Knight's Forester," Flemish or German. Early sixteenth century. The Wallace Collection, Hertford House, London. — 175
11. P. Bruegel, "Two Peasant Women." Berlin-Dahlem, Staatliche Museen. — 188
12. P. Bruegel, "Summer." Hamburg, Kunsthalle. — 194
13. P. Bruegel, "The Blue Cloak." *Netherlandish Proverbs*. Berlin-Dahlem, Staatliche Museen. — 216
14. P. Bruegel, "A Maerte." National Museum, Stockholm. — 226
15. Anon. (Dutch), "Overhand": *The Battle for the Breeches*. — 232

Acknowledgments

The generous support of Loyola Marymount University has helped make this work possible. In particular I wish to thank Dr. Joseph Jabbra, Academic Vice President, Sister Mary Milligan, R.S.H.M., Dean of the College of Liberal Arts, and Professor Linda Bannister, Chair of English, for their support in the form of a Faculty Summer Research Grant, The Eugene Escallier Award for Foreign Travel, and several Raines' Funds awards in support of research assistants. Both Dean Milligan and Prof. Bannister have granted additional and generous support for this publication. The Administratie Kunst, Muziek, Letteren, Podiumkunst, Ministerie van de Vlaamse Gemeenschap, Brussels, has made available generous translation support.

Jackson I. Cope, Joseph A. Dane, and Moshe Lazar oversaw the very early stages of this work. Joseph Dane has continued as a trusted reader and friend. Thanks to my research assistants and former students, Ms. Kami Chisholm, Ms. Janine Gerzanics, and particularly, Ms. Pamela Felcher, for their enduring patience and help. A mathemetician by trade, Michael Berg was nonetheless a vigilant proofreader of Dutch, out-matched only by my mother, Martha A. de Vroom, an elementary school teacher for forty years.

For the support and good humor of friends and family, thanks to: Richard S. Caldwell, Jane Crawford, Thomas A. Hellwarth, William A.D. Hellwarth, Christiane Le Guen, Peter J. Manning, Jennifer Rodes, Margaret Rosenthal, Albert Sonnenfeld, the late Caroline Shaw, Jeffrey S. Siker, Mona Simpson, Johannes de Vroom, Michael de Vroom, Thomas Walsh, and most of all, Elizabeth A. Wolf.

Detail from the *Allegory of Temperance*, by P. Bruegel, "a morality play." Rotterdam, Museum Boymans-van Beuningen.

Introduction

The four plays and six farces of the Hulthem Manuscript are not only the earliest preserved plays in the literature of the Netherlands, they are among the earliest secular plays to survive from the European Middle Ages. The six farces, called "sotternieën," are the earliest known examples of the genre written in the vernacular, while the four "abele spelen," plays of extraordinary breadth, quality and scope, take their place among the anomalous *Le garçon et l'aveugle* (c. 1282), Philippe de Mézières's *L'estoire de Griseldis* (c. 1395), and more generally *Les Miracles de Nostre Dame*, as the first and finest examples of secular drama in the Middle Ages.

The Hulthem Manuscript was copied by one scribe sometime between 1405–1410. The composition of the plays is commonly assigned to the last quarter of the fourteenth century, although some critics put the date earlier — between 1325–1350.[1] The manuscript is named for a judge and a prodigious collector from Gent, Karel van Hulthem, who in 1811 bought at auction this medieval manuscript for the price of five-and-a-half francs. After his death in 1835, the Belgian government bought Hulthem's entire collection (one of the largest private collections in Europe), which is now housed in the Royal Library of Brussels. The Hulthem Manuscript (numbers 15589–15623) has 241 folios, each page containing two columns of text. The codex contains two hundred and ten works, among them: chivalric romances, songs, farces, parables, prayers, fables, miracles, sermons, and various religious works. It is a kaleidoscopic and encyclopedic collection of the various kinds of literature produced in the Middle Ages. Most of the texts in the manuscript are preceded by a title, a number locating them in the collection, and, at the close of each work, a number corresponding to the total lines. In between the various shorter pieces, the collection contains some of the most important literary pieces produced in the Netherlands in the Middle Ages, among them: *Van sente Bradaane; De borchgravinne van Vergi*; the works of Sergher Diengotgaf; the play, *Theophilus*; and the four "abele spelen" and the six farces which accompany them. The *Theophilus*, the "abele spelen," and the farces come to us only because they are preserved in this manuscript.

The Hulthem Manuscript is unusual because it is written on paper and not parchment; it is, therefore, one of the oldest surviving "paper books." The manuscript is not illustrated, the margins are narrow, and the initials at the beginnings of texts are merely functional and not decorative—in other words, it is a rather straightforward and plain reproduction of the texts collected within. These qualities have led scholars to theorize that the codex did not belong to a noble person or patron, but rather that it served as a kind of standard collection for a scriptorium, a sourcebook for copyists. This might further explain why the number of lines is tallied at the end of each work on the grounds that it simplified the calculation of what the copyist would be paid.[2] It has been suggested that the codex belonged to a professional "voorlesere," or "recitor."[3] It may also have belonged to a civic scriptorium, such as the one found in Brussels, where the well-known fourteenth-century copyist, bookbinder and book dealer, Godevaert de Bloc, could have used it to produce books for his clients, among them members of the court of the Duke of Coudenberg.[4]

The general consensus among critics is that the plays and farces of the Hulthem Manuscript were written by a single unknown author (Leendertz, van Mierlo, Stuiveling, etc.).[5] J.J. Gielen sees the overarching theme of the development of romantic love through the four plays as possibly paralleling the developing career of the poet.[6] William van Eeghem has proposed the writer, Jan Dille, the "Ovid of Brussels" as he was called, as the author of the plays. According to van Eeghem, Dille is the only one of twelve known authors alive at the time the plays were written who used the goddess Venus in his work (as the author of the "abele spelen" does in *Vanden Winter*). Dille's close contact with the court and his use of courtly themes in his other works might again, according to van Eeghem, support the theory that he was the author of the "abele spelen."[7] Van Mierlo sharply disagrees.[8]

The generic designation "abel spel" at the start of each of the four plays may point to a single author who added the designation to reinforce the sense that these plays belong together.[9] The broader evidence for a single author includes: the many repeated phrases among the four plays; the similarity of style, theme and syntax as well as various similar plot elements. Beside the similarities of language, tone and sentiment, which many scholars have commented on,[10] the four plays share many other specific similarities. The recognition of an "object" is common in the plays (a portrait in *Gloriant*, a turban in *Esmoreit*, an allegorical tale in *Lanseloet*). All four plays are contructed in ways that divide the plays in two. Each play is set in two countries which are very far apart (Denmark and Rawast; Sicily and Damascus; Bruuyswijc and Abelant) or in the comparable division of the seasons between Summer and Winter. Dialogue and monologue are used in all four plays to bridge the expanses of geography. For example, Reinhout (*Lanseloet*) travels from Denmark to Africa all the while revealing his inner thoughts about finding Sanderijn; Esmoreit reveals his tormented soul to the audience as he travels from his pagan Damascus to Sicily. The religious difference between Moslems and Christians, like the two-part geography of the plays, divides three of the plays into opposing religious sentiments, while similarly in *Vanden Winter*, the two seasons compete for absolute power. Each "abel spel" is essentially constructed around the comic plot of two lovers finding each other, with a "blocking figure" thrown in as an obstacle to their love. Esmoreit and Damiet, Gloriant and Florentijn, Sanderijn and Lanseloet, are variously kept from one another by their parents or parental stand-ins. Summer and Winter, conversely, are kept from destroying each other by Venus. The movement of the plot is always for one of the lovers to cross the divide between them and ultimately bring the other to one place where they can be together. Usually the outcome of the plot sparks a conversion (*Esmoreit* and *Gloriant*), though sometimes, as in the case of Sanderijn in *Lanseloet*, it is not clear. In *Vanden Winter*, it is Moiaert who goes to Venus and persuades her to convince Winter and Summer to convert their war to peaceful coexistence. In each play, a character is punished and/or ostracized: Robbrecht in *Esmoreit*, the Red Lion and his nephew, Floerant, in *Gloriant*, Lanseloet in *Lanseloet*, and (comically) the Cockijn in *Vanden Winter*. Further, in *Esmoreit*, *Lansloet*, *Gloriant* (and to a lesser extent *Vanden Winter*) conversations which are overheard are used to drive the plot forward.[11]

The faithful councilor and messenger is common to all the plays: Platus (*Esmoreit*), Rogier (*Gloriant*), Reinhout (*Lanseloet*), and Moiaert (*Vanden Winter*), as are the remarkably strong and vibrant portrayals of female characters. Interestingly, with the exception of *Lanseloet* (which contains two women characters, one good and one evil) there is only one woman in each of the four plays: Florentijn, Damiet, Venus, and Sanderijn. Their many differences aside, all the heroines of the "abele spelen" are powerful, resourceful, intelligent and essential to the comic outcome of each play.

Despite these similarities (or because these similarities are inconclusive), there are critics who speculate that the plays may have had more than one author and there are also those who are too uncertain to commit themselves either way. Syntactical analyses have prompted G. Stellinga to speculate that while *Gloriant* and *Esmoreit* use similar kinds of sentences in terms of style and structure, *Vanden Winter* and *Lanseloet* are distinctly different in syntactical and structural terms and, therefore, may have been written by a different author.[12] Those critics who are uncertain regarding the single author theory of the plays include: H. Mandos, Garmt Stuiveling and, to some extent, B. Hunnigher and N.C.J. Wijngaards.[13]

The collection of plays found in the Hulthem Manuscript (in particular the "abele spelen"), like Bach's *b-minor Mass* written some three hundred years later, seems to consist of dramatic pieces which are more consistently related than unrelated. These plays seem to belong together, to the same family of subjects and themes, the same kinds of plays, just as the various movements of Bach's *b-minor Mass* seem to belong to the same composition, even though it is unclear whether he ever meant them to. The "abele spelen" are variations, permutations, of the same set of problems, the same world view, written with a consistent and inclusive sensibility. It is perhaps in this sense that the argument for a single author might best be made.

Along with the various theories of authorship come the various theories of the place of composition. The plays were written in "Diets," the literary language of the Netherlands in the Middle Ages, sometimes called Middle Dutch.[14] Critics generally agree that the plays were written somewhere in the southern part of the territory of the Netherlands. Worp suggests, because of what he sees as the French influence in the plays, that they were written in Flanders near the French border;[15] Leendertz cites references in the plays to Flemish place names (Gent and Kortrijk) and swear words ("bij St. Nicolaas") in order to argue for a Flemish provenance.[16] Limburg has been named as a possible place where these plays may have originated[17] though several critics (P. Tack, J.W. Muller and others) have suggested that Brabant is the place where the plays were written.[18] Van Mierlo has argued that the text of the plays was written in Flanders and that the scribe added the several aspects of "Brabantsche" style and language found in the plays.[19] Citing the widespread and rich "Brabantsche" influence, van Loey disagrees, arguing that the accuracy and pervasivness of the Brabant's elements in the plays is evidence that these were not just the finishing touches of a copyist or scribe but the dialect of their author.[20] While most contemporary critics agree that Brabant is the place of composition, van Anrooij and van Buuren have suggested that it was most likely the Brabant of northern Belgium, near Brussels or Leuven with their respective courts and civic populations, where such a collection as the Hulthem Manuscript contains could have found its audience.[21] By contrast, H. Pleij and others have presented evidence that the plays were linked to the influential Franciscans and Minorites of the Southern Netherlands who may have composed them or had them composed for the emerging towns to which they were bound.[22]

Just how the secular plays of the Hulthem Manuscript developed in the southern part of the Netherlands or Flanders has been the subject of much speculation, and again, there are no conclusions which can be said to exclude all others. Moltzer has argued, based on the dialogues which structure so much of the "abele spelen," that these plays developed out of the dialogues commonly found in the texts of minstrels and troubadours.[23] This view is supported by the work of Te Winkel, Ten Brink, Knuvelder and Wijngaards.[24] Worp, pointing to some of the similarities between the "abele spelen" and the *Miracles de Nostre Dame*, concludes that either the secular drama in the Netherlands developed out of the religious drama, as perhaps it did in France, or that secular Netherlandic drama was taken directly from French models, which in turn had developed out of the religious drama, particularly the miracle play.[25] In later discussions, de Vooys, Stuiveling and others have pointed to the importance of Arthurian and courtly motifs in the "abele spelen" and speculated that these plays are dramatized versions of French romances.[26] But discussions of origin and influence concerning early French and Netherlandic texts are common. For example, the cross-fertilization between the various branches of the French medieval beast epic *Le Roman de Renart* and the Netherlandic *Van den Vos Reynaerde* poses similar questions for scholars regarding the problems of influence, origin, and originality between the literature of these two nations.[27] Further, as the work of many scholars suggests (Leendertz, van der Riet, Willems, Knuvelder and van Mierlo), a great deal of uncertainty surrounds these questions of influence and the development of secular medieval drama in the Netherlands. Just how and why secular medieval Netherlandic drama came about when it did, or whether it developed out of religious drama, is unclear. These critics wonder if there was a particular impetus or consciousness, a sensibility, which put the secular drama into motion, gave it momentum and an audience.

Much critical ink has been spent understanding precisely what the generic designation "abel spel," at the beginning of each of the four plays, means. Indeed the definition of "abel" is uncertain.[28] According to Verdam in the *Middelnederlandsche Handwoordenboek*, "abel," like the English word "able," means capable, able, apt and skilled; but it also means dexterous, adroit, beautiful, nice, and exceptional. Critics have suggested many readings of this term ranging from "serious," to "leading toward exemplary morality," to "serious in comparison with the farces which follow."[29]

The generic typing suggested by the various meanings of "abel" might be better determined by looking at the scope of the plays themselves. *Esmoreit, Gloriant* and *Lanseloet* are at once concerned with the development of comedy, whose subject is love and

INTRODUCTION 17

ultimately marriage, as they are with the subjects of tragedy, namely, revenge, punishment, and ultimately death. In these plays the good are rewarded, the bad are punished. And while the names of God, the Virgin, and Christ are invoked, these plays depend on human action, time, and providence to resolve tragedy.[30] The geography of all three plays is vast (often commuting between Europe and the Middle East);[31] and the time which elapses in all three is expansive (enough for the baby born at the start of *Esmoreit* to reach manhood, for Lanseloet's beloved, Damiet, to run away to Africa where she is married and becomes a noble woman, and for several characters to journey between Christendom and the "Pagan lands" with adventure along the way in *Gloriant*).[32] Had these plays been written in England at the beginning of the seventeenth century we would classify them, along with *The Winter's Tale* and *Philaster*, as tragicomedies.[33] The "abele spelen" are stage romances" and they are perhaps the very first examples of tragicomedy as we define the genre much later in the history of European drama.

Scholars had generally thought that "abele spelen" were performed by local groups of amateur actors or members of the circle of professional reciters who performed at local courts.[34] Court accounts indeed frequently refer to reciters, but they seem never to have been paid as performers of plays. According to Max Hermann's work on an edition of Terence's comedies printed in Lyon in 1495, the editor, Jodocus Badius Ascensius (Joost de Bruine of Assche), a Flemish humanist, makes reference to what may have been the performance practice of the "abele spelen."[35] Badius says:

> For this reason masks are used by the performers who, for a remuneration, act out the adventures of kings and ladies in chambers, as we *see everywhere today in Flanders and different neighboring regions*. These performers use different masks so that one performer or actor can play different parts. Another reason for using masks is that sometimes an actor has to play the part of a child and sometimes that of a young man, or a grown man, or an elderly man, or an ancient man, or sometimes that of a king, a lord, a messenger, a farmer, a merchant, a traitor, or a shady character, which makes it necessary to use different masks.[36] [my emphasis]

Both *Esmoreit* and *Lanseloet* require that an actor age from a child to a man over the course of the play. In addition, the doubling of parts, the depiction of particular kinds of characters like the Moslems in *Gloriant* and *Esmoreit*, or the goddess Venus in *Vanden Winter*, for example, would be well served by the use of masks. Willem M.H. Hummelen, following Hermann's lead, uses another passage from Badius (c. 1496) to suggest that by the end of the fifteenth century indoor and professional stage performances were organized, especially for plays with serious subjects, and that an entrance fee was charged:

> Item, that all chamber actors, who have acted out in chambers the histories and chronicles as announced on the banners they usually display, are excluded from participation. Also excluded are actors who, for a reward, have performed farces in such chambers, particularly following the competition at Louvain [in 1498]. On the same terms all persons are excluded from participation who have become professional reciters, verse composers, etc.[37]

Using the Dutch word for "chamber actors" ("camerspelers"), Hummelen is able to link these actors to the masked "joculatores" and make a convincing case that the "abele spelen" were probably performed by "professional masked actors on a stage with a tiring house that had at least two entrances to the front of the stage."[38] Again, as Hummelen argues, the need for various costume changes and entrances to represent the various distant geographies would be well served by a backstage where both costumes and masks could be changed.

Hummelen further suggests that the plays and farces of the Hulthem MS. are divided and preserved in the manuscript in the form of five "'scripts,'—that is, five texts prepared for the production of one or more stage performances. Each script consists of what, for lack of a better term, may be referred to as a primary play (between 625 and 1142 lines in length), followed by a *sotternië* (a short farce, between 111 and 245 lines long)."[39] In other words, Hummelen sees the manuscript as indicating dramatic groupings which would be performed together. Further, according to Hummelen, it is likely that these plays were performed in "Chambers of Rhetoric" because of the directions to the audience in *Gloriant* and *Esmoreit*. In both these plays, the audience is asked to remain quiet and seated at the start of the play and then to descend by the stairs at the end of the play—presumably from the top floor of a municipal hall—further evidence, according to Hummelen, that the "abele spelen" were performed by a group of established, professional, and municipal players.

Along these same lines, recent discussions of the audience of the "abele spelen" have pointed increasingly away from aristocratic and courtly audiences to those composed of "stedelingen," city-dwellers or burgers. J. Beckers has shown that the various editions of *Lanseloet*, especially the Goudse edition of 1486, reveal changes and emendations from the manuscript version. This is particularly the case with the character of Sanderijn, who becomes even more obedient and patient and, therefore, an even more ideal wife in terms of "burgerlijke" values.[40] As I have already noted, the farce which follows each "abel spel" is introduced at the beginning of the play. Van Dijk has shown that the prologues to the plays and the ties between the plays and the farces which follow them could have been adapted to suit a variety of audiences or patrons.[41] An insistence on courtly values in the manuscript version, he concludes, is not fixed. These links could have been tailored to underscore different values from those found in the original version. O.S.H. Lie traces the developing burger morality in *Lanseloet* and concludes that in that play the morality of the older code of courtly love is replaced by the new morality of marriage. The burger/citizen mentality, exemplified by Sanderijn's insistence on love only within marriage, shows the transformation of the ideals of courtly love (Lanseloet's misguided romance) into the new morality of the "stadsliteratuur" of the evolving middle class.[42] According to Lie and Beckers, any of the prologue and epilogue discussions of courtly morality, seemingly addressed to aristocratic audiences, may have been "tacked on;" they may also have been altered for performances because their ideology is quite different from the revisions of "standsverschil" (class difference), love, and courtly language found in the plays themselves. Indeed, all the "abele spelen" (not just *Lanseloet*) are full of middle-class revisions of the older, courtly, and aristocratic values, particularly when it comes to love. In *Gloriant*, as in *Lanseloet*, "burgerlijke" values are maintained. The happy outcome of the lovers' courtly quest for each other is a marriage rooted in Christian spirituality that creates "love among equals," and preserves the state by the promise of children. The same may be said of *Esmoreit* (though perhaps to a lesser extent), where again Christian marriage and the re-establishment of political and personal community is the context for romantic love. *Vanden Winter* in a similar vein is concerned with the replacement of one set of older, mythological beliefs with the "new learning" of the later fourteenth century.[43] H. Pleij's assessment is a good summary of the plays' sensibilities and attitudes, characteristic of the morals of the citizens for whom (and by whom?) they were written: "the atmosphere of the abele spelen is so fittingly courtly as to have been entirely dictated by the self-emancipating bourgeoisie."[44]

Concerning documented, contemporary performances we have some evidence. We know of one performance on August 14, 1412, when a company of actors from Diest, a town in Brabant, came "te wagen en peerde" (by horse and wagon) to Aken and put on, "*het spel van Lanseloet*."[45] This may have been *Lanseloet of Denmark*, which indeed seems to have been the most popular of the plays if we judge popularity by the number of early printed editions. Beside an incunabula printed in Gouda, there are several sixteenth- and seventeenth-century printings of the play, some of them in French and German.[46] Van de Riet has compiled a list of twenty-one books printed in Gent in 1532, among which was contained the "spel van den Hertoghe van Bruisewijc," which he says could be none other than *Gloriant*. This same list includes a "spel van eender Miracule van der Conijnghinne van Cecilien," which may have been *Esmoreit*.[47]

A complete set of the acting parts of Sanderijn and Lanseloet is preserved in the city archives of 'sGravenpolder, dating from the sixteenth century. It seems to have been the property of a "*rederijkerskamer*," one of the several acting companies which were offshoots of the French "*rhétoriqueurs*," companies which flourished in the Low Countries, this one called "De Fiolieren." In this document, beside the part of Sanderijn there is a note, "dese rolle gespeelt op Jaer 1720" (this part acted in the year 1720).[48]

In this volume, the ten collected plays and sotties of the Hulthem Manuscript appear in the same order as they do in the original manuscript, namely *Esmoreit* (1021 lines) followed by the farce, *Lippijn* (200 lines), *Gloriant* (1141 lines) followed by the farce, *De Buskenblaser* (210 lines), *Lanseloet* (954 lines) followed by the farce, *Die Hexe* (111 lines), *Vanden Winter ende Vanden Somer* (626 lines) followed by the farce *Rubben* (245 lines). Two other farces are included in the collection, the fragment *Truwanten*, which begins at line 104 and ends at line 197, and the fragment *Drie daghe here* of which we have only the first 404 lines.

As I have noted, each "abel spel" introduces, either in the opening rubrics or at the close of the play (or in both places), a farce: *Lippijn, De Buskenblaser, De Hexe,* and *Rubben*; each follows a particular play. The fragments *Truwanten* and *Drie daghe here* stand alone, although they may have been separated by a missing play.

All the plays were written in rhymed couplets with the last line of each character's speech made to rhyme with the first line of the next. For example:

GLORIANT: ...
 Boven allen vrouwen, die ic nie sach.
 Ay god, die gheve haer goeden dach,
 Die mi ghesent heeft desen pant.
ROGIER: O hoghe gheboren wigant,
 Ic hebbe mine boetscap ane u ghedaen;
 Nu willic weder keren gaen
 Toter joncfrouwe Florentijn.
GLORIANT: Rogier, Rogier, nu soe moetti sijn ... (v. 301–8)

The verse form is call Old Germanic (*Oudgermaans*) and has four stresses per line, sometimes three, and it is virtually free of iambs, as in the following examples taken from different pieces:

Her Sòmer, dàt wetic hèrde wèl ...
Vanden Winter (v. 68)

Ic hèbbe een quàet wif, als ghì wel wèt ...
Drie daghe here (v. 75)

Wàt, Rùbben. en sìdi dàer?
Rubben (v. 25)

Vroùwe, waeròmme smìtti mì ...
Truwanten (v. 116)

Neither the rhyme scheme nor the verse forms are complex in the "abele spelen." All the "cues" are delivered in complete lines, and there is no rapid-fire dialogue between characters. According to van Dijk, who draws his terms from van den Berg, the versification and rhyme scheme of the "abele spelen" is reinforced by the virtual absence of iambs, making a "quiet" impression.[49]

Esmoreit

Esmoreit is the only one of the "abele spelen" for which an historical source may exist. Peters and later Duinhoven have shown that there may be a correspondence between the characters in the play and actual known persons.[50] Peters has identified the Christian King of Sicily and his Queen with Frederick III of Aragon, King of Sicily 1296–1337, and his wife, Eleonora of Anjou, daughter of Charles II and Maria of Hungary. After Frederick's death, Maria became a Franciscan nun.[51] In this scenario, the villain Robbrecht is Maria's brother, Robert of Anjou, King of Naples 1309–1343, who was a member of the Guelph party[52] and who tried to take over the Sicilian crown because his brother-in-law, Frederick, had no heir. The parallels here to the play are obvious and according to Duinhoven suggest that *Esmoreit* may indeed be older than 1340 and that the text of the play was reworked at least once.[53]

Duinhoven has identified another source of the play, the "*Rijmbijbel*," written by Maerlant, c. 1300, a reworking of a twelfth-century French text, Petrus Comestor's *Historia scolastica*. Both of these works were popular recastings and reworkings of the Vulgate, larded with various apocryphal stories and details.[54] Duinhoven points to the source for *Esmoreit* in passages from Exodus, taken from Maerlant's version of the tale describing Moses' foundling childhood, the prophecy surrounding his birth, his maturation, and his campaign to capture Saba (Ethiopia) when he was still an Egyptian prince. Duinhoven also suggests that the name "Damiet" is a bastardization of a place name in the *Rijmbijbel*, and that "Esmoreit" is a version of Moses, "es moyses," which became "esmores" and then "esmoreit." The name "Esmeré," however, is common to several thirteenth- and fourteenth-century French romances and in *Baudouin de Sebourc, IIIe roy de Jhérusalem*, we find the name "Damiate."[55] Nonetheless, Duinhoven's argument is convincing, especially in the larger scope of the similarities between the Moses story and Esmoreit.

Sources for *Esmoreit* otherwise consist of a more general backdrop of largely French chivalric tales and romances, though no exact source can be named. Scholars have tried in various ways to find and hypothesize sources for the play, but, other than Duinhoven, to little or no avail.[56] Eastern tales about exotic princes who look to the stars for answers are found in such works as the French *Li Dis de l'empereur Coustant*. A somewhat similar tale to that of *Esmoreit* is found in the fifteenth-century *Le Livre de Baudoyn, Conte de Flandre*, which may have been a reworking of an earlier version, but it is not clear. The Netherlandic tale *Jan uut den vergiere* has also been pointed to as a possible source, though some critics disagree.[57] It is clear that *Esmoreit* is familiar, but from where this familiarity derives, unless it be Moses alone, remains uncertain.

The action of *Esmoreit* shifts between two plots and two locations which become intertwined. In Sicily there is a the plot against the newborn heir, Esmoreit. At the same time, in Damascus, the king is told by his astrologer, Platus, that a baby born in the West that night will one day kill him. The two locations and plots are bridged when Platus, with the King of Damascus' consent, rides to Sicily to find the child and bring him back to Damascus where he will be raised "according to our law," which, in theory at least, will prevent the child from ever wanting to kill the king because he will regard him as his father. Meanwhile, in Sicily, the king's brother, Robbrecht, plots to murder the new baby born to his aging brother and his young queen. The cause of Robbrecht's anger is that this child has replaced him in the line of succession, barring him from becoming king when his brother dies. Just at the moment when Robbrecht has taken possession of Esmoreit, Platus rides up and offers to buy the child for a great sum of money. Robbrecht agrees and Platus takes Esmoreit home to Damascus.

In Damascus, Esmoreit becomes the charge of Damiet, the king's daughter, who dotes on him and raises him: "I will gladly be your sister and mother" (v. 283). Back in Sicily, the king and queen are distraught over the disappearance of their son. Robbrecht, in the meantime, convinces the king that his queen has murdered the child herself. Enraged, the king falsely accuses her and has her imprisoned. The scene ends with the queen protesting her innocence.

Eighteen years later we return to Damascus. Esmoreit is walking in an orchard when he overhears Damiet say that he is really not her brother, but a foundling. She goes on to proclaim her romantic love for him. Esmoreit confronts Damiet and decides he must set out in search of his family. Damiet exacts from him the promise that he will one day return to her and then she gives him an embroidered band of cloth in which he was swaddled as an infant, suggesting he wear it on his head as a turban so that someone may recognize him by it.

Esmoreit, crest-fallen because he is an orphan and not a prince as he once believed, goes in search of his parents and "the one who made me a foundling" (v. 607). In Sicily he is recognized by his mother from her prison cell. Soon, he is reunited with his father, who in turn is deeply repentant for having wrongly imprisoned his wife. In the meantime, Damiet convinces Platus to go with her in search of Esmoreit about whom she is worried. They go to Sicily where, reunited, Esmoreit and Damiet renew their love for one another and Robbrecht's villainy is revealed by Platus. The play ends with a family reunited, the prospect of marriage between Damiet and Esmoreit imminent, the hanging of Robbrecht, and the triumphant Esmoreit advising the audience to live virtuously.

Esmoreit combines several familiar tropes. The play contains the story of the calumnized or falsely accused queen,[58] just as it does the plot of the foundling recovered.[59] Another "story" which is imbedded in the play, perhaps a surviving trace or borrowing from the sacred drama, is that of Herod and the slaughter of the innocents. In *Esmoreit*, the astrologer Platus (like the Magi) has seen something in the stars which predicts the birth of a child who is a threat to the Moslem (in place of Hebrew) king. While they do decide to kidnap this child, the King of Damascus, as it turns out, is not a cruel tyrant. Instead, following Platus's advice, the king plans to raise the child so that he will never turn against him. After initial similarities, the Herod figure in the play, the King of Damascus, is displaced by Robbrecht, the cruel brother to the King of Sicily and Esmoreit's uncle. It is Robbrecht who fears Esmoreit will take away his chance to rule, and it is he who plots the child's death in language redolent of the raving and conventionally mad Herod. The displacement of the Herod figure in *Esmoreit* from the King of Damascus to Robbrecht, the king's brother in Sicily, explains in part why Platus' prediction—that Esmoreit would one day kill the King of Damascus—is not fulfilled. It is more than Moslem law and kindness which undercuts Platus' prediction. Esmoreit, in keeping with the prediction, will marry Damiet and she does become a Christian, but his rage and vengeance are saved for the one who made him a foundling and who is the true Herod in the play: Robbrecht. Esmoreit invites the parallel between the King of Damascus and Robbrecht: the former treats the child with love and respect, making him the charge of his own daughter and raising him as his son; the latter kidnaps the child, plans to murder him, and ruins his mother to insure that his brother will have no more children with her.

Esmoreit is a moving account of recovery and recognition which, like its successor *The Winter's Tale*, has the quality of a story dramatized. Of all the "abele spelen," it is the one that "tells well," perhaps because, like *The Winter's Tale*, it is made up of so many familiar and different kinds of stories.

Gloriant

An exact source for *Gloriant* has been hard to pin point. The play, like the other "abele spelen," owes much to the milieu of the chivalric romance. The over-arching themes of the "revenge of Venus," "love divided by distance," or the tale of the knight who captures a Saracen princess and brings her home to be baptized before he marries her, are all commonly found in the traditions of chivalric romances of France, Spain, and the Netherlands.[60] "Valentijf," Gloriant's horse, is found in several chivalric tales, most popularly in the *Chanson de Roland*, and in general "Abelant" is a name for the East. The name the Red Lion, "rouge lion," is found in several romances: *Godefroi de Bouillon, Les Chétifs, Antioche, La Conquête de Jérusalem, Lion de Bourges* and *Baudoin de Sebourg*,[61] the latter sharing several plot elements with *Gloriant*. In *Baudoin de Sebourg*, the old Red Lion is killed by Godfried of Bouillon, and his son goes back to "Abelant," where, like the Red Lion in *Gloriant*, he hates the Christians for murdering his father: "le Prince sarrasin brûlant de venger sur les chrétiens la morte de son père." On his way home he meets Ernout of Beauvais, the Knight of the Swan, who has two sons, Esmeré and Gloriant. In Abelant, the King's daughter, Elienor, falls in love with Esmeré and eventually she is baptized and marries him in Nimae (Nijmegen).[62] Versions of the names the "Hertog of Bruuyswijc" and "Florentijn" are found in several contexts.[63] "Bruuyswijc" may be Brunswijck, a town in Germany close to Brabant, although it may be that Bruuyswijc is a part of France, given the other French place names, Normandy and Auvergne, in the play.[64] In the fables of Flanders, there is a well-known folktale called "Van den hertog van Brunswijk," which has several elements in common with *Gloriant,* among them the use of the lion and the falcon as images, the separation from the beloved, and a journey to the Middle East.[65]

Based on the argument that the "abele spelen" are dramatized versions of portions of epic tales, A.M. Duinhoven has suggested that the point of departure for *Gloriant* is the Middle-Netherlandic *Floris ende Blancefloer.*[66] Arguing that the *Gloriant* which has come down to us in the Hulthem MS. is itself a reduction and a possible corruption of an earlier and more detailed text, Duinhoven methodically details the many general similarities (as well as the differences) between the two works: in both there is a main character who is a young and beautiful woman who depends on the support of an eastern despot, a Moslem. She enters into a relationship with a young Christian prince from the west; she is caught and thereby brings both Moslem and Christian into mortal danger. Her fate was to be beheaded, but at the last moment she is saved.[67] In the general scope of the two works, both are concerned with the juxtaposition of Islam and Christianity; both are explorations of the theme of love divided by distance; in both, the young woman is Islamic and the young man, Christian; and in both the young lovers attest that they share the same times of birth.[68] It is interesting to note that while Duinhoven's work is exacting and detailed in its analysis, he does not argue that *Floris ende Blancefloer* is a source for *Gloriant,* but rather that the reductive nature of the play limits what we can say about its source. Duinhoven postulates that *Gloriant* was initially a dramatized version of an episode from *Floris ende Blancefloer,* but that the original text which links the two pieces — an "original" which would have demonstrated more conclusive evidence of its reliance on *Floris ende Blancefloer* — has disappeared.[69] According to Duinhoven, the surviving *Gloriant* is a faded palimpsest which reveals its inheritance only through careful textual reconstruction and imaginative speculation.

Gloriant, like *Esmoreit* and *Lanseloet*, is, as we have mentioned, set between two distant places, Bruuyswijc (which is Christian and European) and Abelant (which is Moslem and Near Eastern). In the play the hero, Gloriant, refuses to marry because he has never found a woman who is good enough for him. He spurns the advice of his uncle, Gheraert, and his advisor, Godevaert, at the beginning of the play. Gloriant is proud and he thinks, moreover, that he can be a good knight, that he can act nobly and responsibly toward his country, without a wife. The story which then unfolds, as Gheraert and Godevaert predict, is the "revenge of Venus." Gloriant's boasting is soon undercut when a Moslem princess, Florentijn, who also says she can find no equal, sends him her portrait. He is immediately smitten with her, he professes his love for her, and swears his loyalty to her. Gloriant promises Rogier, her messenger, that he will see her before seven weeks pass and makes his plans to journey to Abelant, sending him home with the plea: "Tell the excellent and beautiful lady/ That she preserve her chastity for me/ For the happiness of us both" (v. 322–5). Gheraert and Godevaert tell Gloriant not to go to Abelant because the Red Lion, Florentijn's father, is their sworn enemy. But Gloriant ignores their warning, protesting his love for Florentijn. He concludes: "I will ride disguised/ As a knight errant./ I will overcome the trials of love" (v. 508–10).

Gloriant arrives in Abelant; the lovers pledge their love to one another; and almost immediately thereafter they are discovered and imprisoned. Rogier comes to the rescue, releases Gloriant, who then lies in wait for the moment of Florentijn's execution as an occassion for her rescue. The couple returns to Bruuyswijc amid much joy and celebration. Gheraert closes the play, commending his nephew, "You have/ Learned to build love's orchard" (v. 1117–8).

In *Gloriant* "love among equals" is the tenor of the relationship between Gloriant and Florentijn. A similar idea is presented in *Lanseloet*, although there the consequences for the hero are tragic. While at the beginning of the play Gloriant boasts that he has found no equal among women, Lanseloet tells his mother he loves Sanderijn despite her low station, arguing "That love seeks her equal/ Even if one is poor and the other rich" (v. 215–6). In other words, Lanseloet says he loves Sanderijn despite their economic and aristocratic inequality because they are equals in love.[70] In a similar way, Gloriant finds his equal in Florentijn, for whom he is willing to risk his life and his reputation. While *Gloriant* may at some level be an exposition of the theme "the revenge of Venus," the hero is quickly able to find his footing in the service of his beloved. In this sense, Gloriant may be justified (as Florentijn seems to be) in his boasting at the beginning of the play. While at first he seems to be a boorish snob, going very far in his refusal to marry and procreate, he also has not found his equal among women, and when he does we are sympathetic because the quest to find her is dangerous, the risk to rescue her, life-threatening— all this confirming that, given "love among equals," anything is possible.

There are two monologues, one by Gloriant and the other by Florentijn, which reconstruct the courtly love portrayed throughout the play. Before he reaches Abelant, Gloriant, in an emotional outpouring, describes the effect of love on him (v. 568–603, repeated again in v. 828–53). Here he tells how love has overtaken him and then he makes an analogy to God, who was also moved by love to take on a human form and suffer. The underlying message is that love is so powerful that even God was subjected to it. The monologue goes on to speak of the power of love in language that is similar to the spiritual, mystical ecstasy expressed by Netherlandic writers like Hadewijch and Beatrijs of Nazareth, who also viewed the workings of divine *minne* as powerful, painful, and all encompassing. Gloriant's tone and description could be theirs:

> O God, what wonder you caused,
> All of it emanating from true love!
> That's why those who know love's ways
> Don't discourage me,
> Even though love causes me so much pain.
> For love is so powerful,
> That she made the strong and almighty God
> Descend from heaven
> To pay our debt for us. (v. 586–94)[71]

The once haughty Gloriant is conquered and overwhelmed by the power of love, a very different man from the one who began the play with: "I know no woman on earth/ With whom I'd like to spend my life" (v. 100–1).

A parallel, but rather different kind of religious monologue is delivered by Florentijn just before she is to be executed (v. 1017–24 and 1033–46). This is Florentijn's farewell to the world in which she shows she has become a very good Christian, although one might wonder when and how this conversion took place since she has had no other contact with a Christian but Gloriant and that only for at most a few hours. Nonetheless, she seems well-versed in the historical details of her new faith:

> God, who was born of a Virgin,
> And who suckled her for food,
> And then patiently endured
> Being taken by the foul Jews,
> And hung on a cross
> On which he died a bitter death
> To bring us everlasting bliss,
> Have mercy on my soul. (v. 1017–24)

While in this passage and in her subsequent pious embracing of Christianity when she is about to be executed, she seems to overdo it a bit when it comes to religious sentiment (in particular in relation to the rest of the play), Florentijn's speech is significant because it makes her more equal in the eventual marriage between herself and Gloriant. She must be a Christian and, thinking she is about to die, she embraces her faith. What we have seen is that for both Gloriant and Florentijn, religion and love have become intertwined: for Gloriant in terms which recall the mystical tradition of the *Brautmystiek*; for Florentijn, in a straightforward lesson on the facts of the faith.[72] In this secular study of "love among equals," what the play insists upon more than any of the other "abele spelen" is the characters' realization of their reliance upon, and similarity of their love to, their faith. For both lovers, the expression of love is fused with the religious sentiment not only of the Middle Ages but of the emerging burger mentality at the end of the fourteenth century. The play insists on the replacement of the courtly ideal (refusals to love, ideals found in portraits, dangerous quests) with a marriage "among equals," dependent on a true understanding of love, which is spiritual (Gloriant) and biblical (Florentijn). The necessity of Gloriant's marriage, in part to create "Children for the good of our country," voiced by Gheraert and Godevaert at the outset of the play moves the play away from older courtly and aristocratic values to those of a "stadsliteratuur."

Lanseloet of Denmark

Lanseloet is arguably the finest and most sophisticated of the "abele spelen." Critics have proposed several sources for the story of the knight, Lanseloet, who falls in love with a Sanderijn, a young woman in the service of his mother.[73] Leendertz was the first to point to the biblical tale of Amnon and Thamar (Samuel 2:13) as the source for parts of the story, particularly the cruelty of Lanseloet's mother.[74] G. Kazemier suggests that the motif of Lanseloet's illness is taken from a Danish ballad (hence Lanseloet van Denemerken) and that the play is a combination of the ballad, the Biblical tale, and Chrétien de Troyes' version of the Lancelot story in *Le chevalier de la charrete*.[75] Duinhoven has argued that the source of the play can be found in the various versions of the prose-Lancelot and that Lanseloet of Denemerken is really "Lancelot van den mere," or Lancelot du lac, who in various versions shares characteristics with his Netherlandic cousin: a feigned illness, and the love both for and of a servant girl.[76] This argument has been hotly contested by G. Kazemier.[77] Lanseloet's view that "love always finds its equal" (210–23) is taken, according to O.S.H. Lie, directly from a popular treatise on love also contained in the Hulthem Manuscript, called *Vander feesten een proper dinc*.[78] Its "courtly ideals" (similar to those which Lanseloet explains to his mother — even though he cannot achieve them) emphasize equality between lovers as essential to true love. In the treatise, true love is blind to the "standsverschil," or class difference, which ultimately prevents Sanderijn from returning Lanseloet's love.[79]

The play begins as Sanderijn spurns Lanseloet's advances even though she seems to love him. Because of their difference in class, Sanderijn is sure Lanseloet can and will never marry her. Lanseloet tries to assure her otherwise, but to no avail. Lanseloet's mother, who overhears their conversation, tells her son that he is foolish to

INTRODUCTION 31

care for a girl so low-born as Sanderijn. Lanseloet does not agree, and in a moment similar to Gloriant's description of "love among equals," Lanseloet defends his feelings for Sanderijn to his mother. Despite his attempt at nobility, however, Lanseloet is weak. Unlike his namesake, the Lancelot of the chivalric tales, this Lanseloet easily forgets himself and quickly falls prey to his mother's secret intentions: to destroy Sanderijn. His mother convinces him that she will get Sanderijn to join him in his room where she will "be in your power" on the condition that he then speak some cruel words to her when he is done with her. Lanseloet agrees, excusing what he will do with the adage: "Many men say things they don't mean" (v. 268).

His mother tricks Sanderijn, who goes to Lanseloet's room, thinking he is ill, furnishing the occasion for him to rape her.[80] When next we see her, Sanderijn is mourning what has happened to her. She wanders far and arrives in Africa, where by a fountain she stops to drink. There a knight who has been hunting all day without success finds her and immediately proposes his love to the "beautiful maid" and asks her to marry him. She tells him that she wants to talk to him, "And please understand my reasoning" (v. 488).[81] Sanderijn goes on to tell a fable of sorts about a high-born falcon who picks one flower from a tree full of blossoms and never again picks another. She ends her tale with the question: "Should the tree then be hated ever after/ And should it be felled and deserted?" (v. 503–4). The knight understands her story, with a moving rejoinder:

> Noble woman, I understand you exactly,
> One flower is nothing,
> So long as no others will be taken.
> For this I cannot possibly hate the tree,
> Nor fell it, nor desert it,
> For it grows so beautifully.
> I see so many flowers blooming on this tree
> In great bunches, impossible to count,
> Which shall produce noble fruit,
> If God permit it.
> From now on, no more talk of this,
> Come with me, truly beautiful wife. (v. 508–19)

Sanderijn goes off to marry the knight and, as she later tells us, lives happily with him. In the meantime, Lanseloet is truly lovesick. He feels he will die if he doesn't find Sanderijn again, so he calls his friend and vassal Reinhout and sends him to search for her.

Reinhout arrives outside the castle where Sanderijn and her husband live. The comic exchange between Reinhout and "The Knight's Forester" that ensues reflects the "comic" (i.e., happy) atmosphere of the place where Sanderijn and her husband now live. After some exchange, the forester agrees to bring Sanderijn to speak to Reinhout. She comes and after much pleading on Reinhout's part (some of it quite patronizing), he realizes that she will never leave her husband whom she truly loves. Reinhout asks Sanderijn to send back something with him to Lanseloet as proof that he has seen and spoken to her. Sanderijn then tells once more the tale she told her husband about the falcon and the tree full of blossoms. Only this time, when she comes to the end of the story, she says:

> Soon thereafter, the falcon came again
> And he sought the branch up and down,
> But he could not find her.
> And because he could not find the branch
> The falcon suffered greatly. (v. 808–12)

Reinhout goes home to Lanseloet and tells him that Sanderijn is dead. When Lanseloet asks for proof that Reinhout has seen her, he repeats the fable. Lanseloet is devastated; he recognizes the fable as a thinly veiled version of what happened between them, and he dies with the delusion that he will be reunited with his beloved in heaven. Reinhout ends the play encouraging every man to "speak courteously and truly" (v. 950), "especially to all women" (v. 949).

In Roemans and van Assche's important preface to their 1963 edition of *Lanseloet*, the authors comment:

> *Lanseloet* is een *tragedie* waarin de held ten onder gaat door eigen falen. Hij was te zwak om weerstand te bieden aan zijn eigen hartstocht, te zwak om het oneerlijke voorstel van zijn moeder af te wijzen, te zwak om de gevolgen van zijn daad moedig te dragen: hij jammert, hij weeklaagt, hij vervloekt zijn moeder als de enige

INTRODUCTION 33

schuldige... en hij sterft. Er is dan ook geen reden om de hoofdfiguur naast de titelrol te zoeken en Sanderijn op de voorgrond te plaatsen. Het stuk begint en eindigt met een monoloog van Lanseloet, het tragische hoofdpersonage.

[*Lanseloet* is a *tragedy* in which the hero falls because of his own failings. He was too weak to resist his own passions, too weak to resist the unfair proposition of his mother, too weak to bear the consequences of his deed: he cries, he laments, he blames his mother as the only guilty one ... and then he dies. There is, therefore, no need to look for any other person beside the main character and to place Sanderijn in the foreground. The play begins and ends with a monologue by Lanseloet, the tragic protagonist.][82]

It seems to me that Roemans and van Assche miss the point here. Indeed they are right about Lanseloet's character and failings, but the power of the play lies precisely in the two outcomes it offers: tragedy for its hero, but comedy for its heroine, complete with a rise in station, marriage, and the promise of children. In the character of Sanderijn we are offered several radical propositions, none the least of which is that a woman who has been raped need not enter a convent, kill herself, or be killed by her family (the usual alternatives), but can live to love again and to achieve power and stature. She can find a man who, in her own words, "gives me all his respect" (v. 757). While Sanderijn's station at the end of the play is not entirely clear, she is the wife of a great knight who keeps a court and has a large castle. She seems to have risen above her class and she has found true love, which she describes in elevated, passionate and complex terms:

> I have married a nobleman
> Whom I love above life itself
> And I do not want to leave him.
> Even if Lanseloet were as rich
> As Hector of Troy;
> Even if God had allowed him
> To wear the same crown
> Alexander wore,
> I still would not choose him.
> I would rather have my husband
> Who gives me all his respect.
> To him I will always be blissfully loyal. (v. 747–58)

and:

> For I have never seen a man on earth
> Whom I honor more
> Than my dear husband.
> It is right because he truly deserves it.
> He is a knight with a great reputation.
> He is a valiant knight, of proud demeanor,
> Well-born and rich in wealth.
> He is prudent and he is wise.
> He is good with weapons,
> And he has done great deeds.
> My heart loves him faithfully and
> Above all creatures. (v. 769–80)

What she leaves out of this description, and what we have witnessed, is that the most important thing about her husband is that he understands the story of the falcon and the blooming bough. That story which Sanderijn tells and retells twice more during the course of the play is an account of what has happened to her; it is the declaration of her rape. Couched in courtly and poetic terms, the tale is remarkable because, while it is an admission of being raped, it is also a subtle rewriting of the traditional implications and consequences of rape. The example she offers puts her rape in a context in which it would be hard to think that she should be punished for "losing a single blossom." When she poses the question, "Should the tree then be hated ever after/ And should it be felled and deserted?" (v. 503–4), it is impossible to deny the meaning and sentiment of her fable and say "yes." Further, the refrain, yet "the tree . . . was full of blossoms," means (what her future husband understands) that there are still countless blooms to pick which will bear fruit. In other words, the fable asserts that virginity is one flower of many. This is truly a liberal and wise notion coming from a serving girl at the end of the fourteenth century.

The story of the falcon and the bough is told twice more in the play, but now it is no longer as an explanation of Sanderijn's rape. When the story is retold it becomes the justification of her refusal to leave her husband and return to Lanseloet. The fable now redresses and rewrites what Lanseloet said to her after he had raped her, in his own description: "such beastly things/ The like of which I have never heard" (v. 250–1). What he said was,

> "I have had enough,
> Sanderijn, I'm stuffed,
> I've gorged myself
> As if I'd eaten seven slabs of bacon." (v. 240–3)

While it is difficult to appreciate the exact vulgarity of this statement in translation, it is clear that she is undeserving of such words, that they are contemptible, even brutish. O.S.H. Lie has pointed out that when Lanseloet speaks these words, he undercuts himself; he is no longer a high-born knight but a low-class "boerenpummel" who does not know what love is.[83] In comparison, what Sanderijn says in return is elevated, genteel and encoded, so that only Lanseloet will understand it. After the rape, Lanseloet pushed Sanderijn away and uttered the cruel words above; in the mirror image of this moment Sanderijn's version says that after the falcon took the bloom, "He began to beat his wings/ And he flew away in great haste" (v. 805–6). She rewrites Lanseloet's cruel words with a version of her own which emphasizes the eagle's desertion of the bough and, thereby, Lanseloet's culpability.

This fable, which first functioned as a way to explain what had happened to her future husband and, conversely, allowed him to reveal his understanding and compassion for her, now becomes the measure of Lanseloet. Sanderijn changes the end of the fable. In place of the question she put to her husband, "should it [the tree] be felled and deserted?" Sanderijn substitutes,

> Soon thereafter, the falcon came again
> And he sought the branch up and down,
> But he could not find her.
> And because he could not find the branch
> The falcon suffered greatly. (v. 808–12)

In this version of the tale, the loss is not the bough's but the falcon's — it is he who has lost the tree, the bough, and with it the blossoms. With this careful alteration, Sanderijn has rewritten her own misfortune and turned it into Lanseloet's. What began as a tale of rape reconsidered is now a tale of the beloved lost forever with Lanseloet as the unrequited and suffering lover. In this sense,

Sanderijn's tale to Lanseloet is retributive: "what you have done to me, you have really done to yourself."

Reinhout's desire to protect Lanseloet and his kinsmen from destruction (v. 825–30) by reporting that Sanderijn is dead produces the final irony and even justice in the play. Lanseloet dies grieving but certain he will be reunited with Sanderijn in the afterlife:

> I hope to see her in heaven,
> And in that hope I die.
> O, merciful God of heaven's kingdom,
> Now receive her soul and mine
> For I am finished with life. (v. 926–30)

The deluded knight dies, thinking not only that he is counted among the saved, but that Sanderijn may finally be his in heaven. But Sanderijn is alive and well, enjoying earthly happiness at the end of the play.

Vanden Winter ende Vanden Somer

This play is the most stylized and yet the least complex of the "abele spelen" because of its structure, a *débat*, and because its characters are allegorical figures much like those found in pieces like the *Roman de la Rose*. As Wijngaards has argued, the simplicity of the play may be because it developed from an oral and folk tradition of storytelling and in the process became a "strijdsdialoog," and then with a few touches, it developed into the play found in the manuscript.[84] In the play, Summer and Winter debate their virtues with a cast of supporters or seconds on either side who argue for the merit of one season over the other. The supporting characters have names like Loiaert (the lazy one), Moiaert (the pretty boy), Clappaert (the loud mouth), and Bollaert (the wind bag). The discussion, which, rises to the level of a duel, concerns the question: "Which season is best suited for love?" Evidence is given on both sides. The Summer argues that in summertime mankind is warm and happy, rolling freely in the grass amid the flowers, easily able to enjoy the fruits of love. Winter and his supporters, on the other side, argue that to make love in winter time is much better and easier because so many people snuggle up together to keep warm every day that love-making is naturally built into the course of events. While the two main characters seem to be mirror images of each other, the play makes some slight and predictable distinctions between them. Summer is portrayed as the more noble and courtly character, while Winter is threatening, harsh, and ill-mannered.

As the play progresses, the argument soon turns to a challenge, with the duel set for an appointed time the next morning. In the meantime, Moiaert, who himself sides with Summer, is concerned about the outcome of such a contest. He fears that if either "Lord" is vanquished, life on earth will change drastically, speculating as he does that "a quarter of the year will be lost in this duel" (v. 414). Moiaert goes to Lady Venus and asks her to serve as arbitress of the duel because, after all, she is the cause of the argument. Venus agrees. The next morning she arrives and with dispatch and delicacy convinces the two sides that each cannot exist without the other, that the two are natural opposites which keep the world in balance: "Each will work according to his nature" (v. 576). The play ends with a disgruntled Cockijn (who was sure Summer would have destroyed Winter had he been allowed to) walking away to find a comfortable place to wait out the winter.

The play has a structure similar to the Aesop fable, *The Sun and the Wind*, where elements like summer and winter strive to see who has the most power, only to conclude eventually that they are equals. According to several critics, the play has its roots in two traditions: one, learned and classical; the other, oral and folk, along the lines of the "jaartijdspelen."[85] Van Dijk has suggested that Venus departs from the older, mythological explanation for the seasons following each other and instead argues her case with evidence which is based on "the new learning" rooted in astronomical and "scientific" evidence, an argument which has been contested by K. van de Warden.[86] K. Iwema has shown that the role of Venus is usually absent as the arbitrator in classical models for this play and instead "ratio" or "wisdom" is often the judge. She concludes that the use of Venus may be an interpolation from popular texts.[87] The critic, van der Poel, takes this argument further by citing various examples from medieval stories, poems, and songs whose subject is love and in which Venus acts as judge of a debate on the subject of love.[88] The general argumentative quality of the piece is reminiscent of the tradition of the academic "disputatio," or the arguments between the prophets and the Jews which are found in medieval plays such as the *Jeu d'Adam* or the *Ludus Nativitatae* from Benediktbeuren. By contrast, the combat between the seasons as echoed in works as various as the myth of Demeter and Persephone and *Sir Gawain and the Green Knight* is found in many versions which are in turn associated with fertility rites, or rites of initiation and passage. *Vanden Winter* links together argument, fable, and fertility rite in a combination which sets this play apart from the other three "abele spelen." On the one hand, *Vanden Winter* is the most rigidly constructed and erudite play of the four "abele spelen"; it is after all a dramatized argument, full of courtly language, mythological overtones, and rhetorical set pieces. On the other hand, the play asks the most basic of questions, "what is the best time for love?" In *Vanden Winter* this question is arbitrated by the goddess Venus but its outcome is of concern only to "common folk"; they are the ones who are most affected by the "Lords" Winter and Summer in the play. These "common folk" (and not, for example, Honesty, Beauty or Well-seeming) are themselves portrayed as "types" in the allegorical landscape of the play. In this sense, the construction and dependence of the characters on "types" puts *Vanden Winter* much closer in sentiment, subject, character, and scope to the farces contained in the manuscript than the other "abele spelen." Like this play, the farces depend entirely on character types: the hen-pecked husband, the plotting mother-in-law, the dull-witted husband, the bossy mistress, and they are almost entirely constructed around arguments between husband and wife (or their "seconds," i.e., Rubben's mother-in-law, Lippijn's wife's girlfriend, and so forth) on the subject of love. Like the fable-quality of *Vanden Winter*, the farces have a penchant for moralizing conclusions like, "A drunk deserves a shrew for a wife," or "Love easily makes man her fool." They are concerned, for the most part, with the same question, only framed in different and domestic terms: "What is the right time for love?"[89]

The Farces

Lippijn

Lippijn has something in common with *De Buskenblaser* and *Rubben*, particularly the motif of the older man married to a younger and adulterous wife. It is the story of a hen-pecked husband whose wife claims to spend all day at mass when really she's out with her lover. One day, Lippijn sees his wife and her lover "in the act." Just as he's thinking how best to punish her, he runs into her girlfriend, Trise, who, through some fast talk, convinces Lippijn to return home where, she says, he'll find his wife sitting by the hearth. Further, she tells Lippijn that what he saw was the work of the devil, or perhaps a fairy. When Lippijn returns home with her, sure enough, his wife is there sitting by the fire. When Trise tells her girlfriend about what Lippijn had accused her of, the wife becomes enraged and threatens to beat and trample him. Lippijn begs for mercy and the farce ends with Lippijn getting beaten by the two women. Lippijn is the perfect cuckold for he is not only old, but he is stupid and so seems to deserve his pummeling at the end of the farce.[90]

Like Rubben, Lippijn is gullible and hen-pecked, and at the same time he would rather believe that his wife is faithful (if shrewish) than that she is adulterous. The conclusion of *Lippijn* is of some interest where an unnamed character (perhaps Lippijn) speaks to the audience in the epilogue:

> Dear friends, we have
> Played for you a farce.
> There are those—you know well—
> Who have seen something like this.
> You know that many funny things like this are seen
> About which nothing more is said.
> Therefore I hope that you truly have found
> Meaning in our little jokes. (v. 185–92)

In this farce, which so clearly makes Lippijn out to be a fool, this ending adds a nice touch of irony: who among us has not seen "something like this, about which nothing more is said?" Who among us do not worry about our wives?

De Buskenblaser "The Box-Blower"

De Buskenblaser is certainly the most vulgar of the farces, with some resemblance in subject and tone to Chaucer's *Miller's Tale* (older husband, younger wife, clerk as lover, a con, and scatological jokes). In the farce, an ugly, gray-haired, spurned and hen-pecked husband is swindled because he wants to turn his gray hairs black so he will seem young to his young wife and she will desire him once more. In exchange for all the money he has gotten for his cow at market (and his change purse too) he is given a small box to blow into, which unbeknownst to him, is filled with soot. He blows into the box and, thinking himself a new man, he returns home, expecting his wife to be astonished and aroused. Upon his arrival he discovers his folly and finds that neither his wife nor his neighbor is sympathetic. His neighbor, naively, suggests he put his head into a bag of urine and clay, the kind traditionally used to clean and remove the oil from wool. His wife adds that she wished he'd have jumped in a "shit hole" himself, instead of having spent their money so stupidly. Enraged, the husband counters by reminding his wife about the money she spent on a lollard passing by with whom he saw her *in flagrante delecto*. The farce ends with a fight.

In an article by van Dijk, Kramer and Tersteg, the authors (following earlier work by H. Pleij) point out that this farce has a great deal in common with a popular medieval exemplum contained in collections used by preachers to illustrate their sermons:

> It should be noted that the devil is a magician who, because he wants to get everyone in his audience laughing, blows into a little box which contains some dirt, and yet he never seems to get dirty. When he passed his little box around to other people, they also didn't seem to get dirty after they had blown into the box. Finally he gives the little box to a fool to blow in, and [the devil] turns toward him the side where the dirt is, and when he blows suddenly there comes out of the box some jet black stuff which makes his whole face black and dirty. Because of his confusion and contamination, all the bystanders start to laugh and applaud. This is how the devil works: if a fool wants to sin in secret, he will, as it were, bring the box of dirt to him.[91]

These exampla furnished the materials for many medieval dramatic pieces including *De Buskenblaser*. Pleij has commented on a version of this exemplum, suggesting that the *Buskenblaser* has religious implications, that it is a didactic text taken from folktales which could expound the devil's workings to simple folk in the context of a sermon.[92]

Van Dijk, Kramer, and Tersteg argue that the monologue which begins the play by "the one man" is typical of the thirteenth-century French monologue, "l'homme à tout faire," "die man die alles kan," "the man who can do everything."[93] The "one man's" bragging "I can ... I can ..." is, of course, ironic because the entire farce is based on the one thing he cannot do: satisfy his wife.

There are several "types" in the play of which the dupe, "the one man," is an ugly, old, stupid "boer," who has just sold his cow at market (he has money in his pocket), he's had a drink or two, and he is married to a young and adulterous wife. Then there is the "second man," a mountebank, a charlatan, a magician (like the devil) who has come to prey on him. The types found in this farce, according to van Dijk, Kramer and Tersteg, mirror the types of speakers found in the earlier French monologues who traditionally fall into the categories of "charlatan" or "herbier" (like "the second man") or "valets" (like the "one man").[94]

The farce is, in essence, a dramatization of unequal love, a kind of dramatic charavari that is tied to the monologues of "l'homme à tout faire," because their subjects also included the ridicule of unequally married couples.[95] In *De Buskenblaser* the inequality between husband and wife is indeed the engine which drives the farce. Following Pleij's lead, van Dijk, Kramer and Tersteg concur that folk traditions of ridicule such as these might indeed have supplied the Franciscan preachers of the southern Netherlands with substantial material for their sermons.[96]

The running joke in this farce is scatological in nature. When the husband, "the one man," begins the play by offering his services for hire to anyone in the audience, he says he's good at lots of things, "And I can dig a fine hole for you" (v. 23). The actual box blowing episode involves blowing into a little box which he thinks will make him desirable, when really it turns him black. The lines themselves imply the joke:

> He put a little box to my lips
> Into which I blew with all my might,
> And out of it came such a force
> That it made me into the beautiful creature you see before you.
> (v. 114–8)

The cure for his blackness is variously suggested by his neighbor and wife, mentioned above, as involving excrement and urine. His wife refers to him several times as dirty, and finally, in the last description of his wife's infidelities, the joke has come full circle. Referring to her sexual activities with the Lollard, the husband says:

> I saw the scum-bag lying on top of you
> I saw him with his tenderloin up your ass,
> And he lay flat out, not sideways,
> I saw it really well, what you two did. (v. 189–92)

to which his wife counters:

> God damn you for the foul bastard you are,
> We had a pretty good time of it! (v. 199–200)

and he answers:

> O yeah? Well it didn't do much
> For me, your little game. (v. 201–2)

Here the joke of the *Buskenblaser* cuts even deeper and dirtier turf, her transgression is "in his face" and he sees it; the real "soot" of the "box" comes into view for all to see and laugh at. In the obscene pun on "doosje," on which the "busken" is based, the underlying truth of this marriage between unequals is retold: when the old husband has sex with his young wife, he is turned into a fool. The episode of the *Buskenblaser* in this sense is of course nothing more than an extrapolation of his foolishness.[97]

Die Hexe "The Witch"

This is perhaps the simplest of all the farces, and certainly at 111 lines it is the shortest. Two women, Machtelt and Luutgaert, complain to each other about their bad luck and decide that it must be the devil who has cursed them. Together they decide to confront another old crone, Juliane, who sells butter and beer by the side of the road and whom they suspect of having caused them trouble because she has a shady reputation. They go to her and ask her for advice, claiming they want to "come into property." She gives them an ironic answer implying that only thieves can get rich quickly. Her two inquisitors miss the humor (and the point) and take what she says to be a proof of her diabolical enterprise. The farce ends with all three fighting, the two women beating Juliane with pots of beer.

Die Hexe is a humorous vignette in which the cure for domestic misfortune is nothing less than the discovery and purging of the forces of evil. As such, it ridicules the superstitions which may have explained the "bad luck" of these two ladies trying to move away from the superstitious explanation of evil in an age which was clearly still quite attached to it. Vromans has shown that *Die Hexe* is composed of various folk traditions and legends about witches and devils strung together to make the farce.[98] They include: cows loosing their milk (v. 24); the devil as "that tomcat from hell" (v. 26); the intersection of two roads as the place where evil dwells (v. 31); Juliane selling butter (v. 38) (it was thought that butter was often churned and needed by witches to help them digest their spice-laden diets); the German beer (v. 73) that Juliane sells, thought to have medicinal and even magic qualities; and lastly, the "hand of a thief" (v. 97), thought to make robbers invisible or to put their victims into a trance. The foolishness of Machtelt and Luutgaert, however, ridicules these folk legends, showing just how willy-nilly they are used to interpret misfortune. In this farce, it is the discrepancy between the domestic troubles (cows not producing milk, butter not clotting) and their solution (revenge on a servant of the devil) in the minds of two simple women that produces the humor and irony.

Rubben

The plot of *Rubben* is one of the most common plots of farce: a man finds his wife delivered of a child he clearly could not have fathered. Rubben begins the play with a monologue describing his predicament. He has been married for three months when his wife is delivered of a child. But he swears he's not the father, "She must have started this [baby]/ Long before I took her as my wife" (v. 19–20). When Rubben is finished, his mother-in-law appears, and, through an elaborate and crooked argument, she convinces him (with the reluctant help of her own husband, Gosen) that he has counted the months incorrectly. Further, she argues that her daughter came to the marriage bed with explicit sexual knowledge and technique, not from experience, but from what she'd heard from others. Rubben returns repentantly to his wife, but not before he has promised to cook supper for his parents-in-law. The play ends with some wry and sharp jabs from Gosen to his wife about the supposed chastity and honesty of women, in particular the two in his immediate family.

Rubben is talked out of the truth by his mother-in-law largely because he is foolish and gullible. But the key to his change of heart is flattery. After she advances arguments about miscounting and after she defends her daughter's chastity, Rubben's mother-in-law tells him that her daughter was skilled in the art of love because, "She thought it was your due;/ . . . It was this great love which ruled her,/ Therefore she could not hide her feelings [for you]" (v. 167, 175–6). It is this argument that Rubben cannot resist: that his wife desires him and that therefore she is a good lover. The argument is enticing because it flatters him, because he brings out the best in her, and because she is passionate for him alone, while at the same time it masks the fact that his wife has born a child after only three months of marriage. What was at issue at the start of the play, the fear that "my wife desired/had sex with, someone else" has disappeared and been replaced by, "my wife desires me alone and therefore she is good in bed." The idea that "she is good in bed because she desires me alone" is illogical since her expertise is based on experience. And yet Rubben is duped. This is what his mother-in-law knows; namely, that men will always be fooled if they think a woman desires them.

Truwanten

This fragmentary farce is missing the first 103 lines, running to 197 lines total. In its complete form it would have been comparable in length to *Lippijn* (200 lines) and *De Buskenblaser* (210 lines). In the farce, a serving girl, the "maerte," is chastised by her mistress for laziness, specifically for letting the farm animals go hungry. The "maerte" protests and quits her job to take up with "Brother Everaet," a corrupt member of a mendicant order. The "maerte" becomes "Sister Luutgaert," and the two take up truancy, living the wandering life of lollard and beguine gone astray. The farce ends with an epilogue told by the devil, who knows that one day he will have all those who "truant" and prey on the shames and sins of others, "hopping about around my kettle."

INTRODUCTION 45

"Lollard" was a term of ridicule for the begging orders, deriving from the Netherlandic "lollen" or "lullen," meaning mumbled prayers or slow singing, which also comes to mean both "fucking" and/or "bullshitting." This view is exemplified by a couplet which survives from the late fifteenth century: "Lulhardi lollant ut numos undique tollant/ Ut reynhart volcures sic lolhart fallit milieres" (Lollards "lullen"[99] to fill their pockets/ Just as Reynard [catches] the chickens, lollards catch the women [my translation].[100] The stereotype of the Lollard in the Middle Ages was that he was hypocritical, out for money, and eager to enjoy carnal relations with women. In the Middle Ages there were three kinds of Lollards, *"paperes pueruli," "willige arme,"* the male version of the Beguines or *"swesters"* (Latin *swestriones*); those who lived in communities in the cities; those who lived outside the cities in communities, *"woud broeders"*; or those who were wandering beggars, *"gyro vagi."* It was also common, as in the case of Brother Everaet, for communal Lollards (in his case, a *woud broeder*) to "defect" to wandering. In Everaet's case, he changes further from a wandering Lollard to a pilgrim, also a common disguise of plain beggars in the Middle Ages. Brother Everaet and Sister Luutgaert fit the profile of fake beggars who claim they have been to Rome and Jerusalem as pilgrims and wear a "souvenir" on their mantle and carry a walking stick to distinguish themselves as pilgrims.[101] The stereotypical Lollard was a lady's man with a worldly appetite, while the stereotypical Beguine was a lusty, young girl. These types were, as in *Truwanten*, often called Brother Everaet and Sister Luutgaert (or Sister Lute). The church was suspicious of the Lollards and nervous because they were spreading heresy among the people.

R.E. Lerner has argued that *Truwanten* is a dramatization for didactic purposes of a passage from Paul's Second Epistle to Timothy.[102] In this vein, Pleij has argued that *Truwanten* may be a dramatized biblical lesson set in the language of the common people and, like *De Buskenblaser*, is taken from a book of sermon topics.[103] This farce has a moral tone at the end, however playfully told, that sets it apart from the other "sotternieën," causing some critics to questions whether it is a farce at all.[104] At the end of the play, it is predicted that the sly and cunning Brother Everaet will meet his match, someone who will eventually outsmart him. The devil's moralizing epilogue indeed bolsters the argument that the play contains the religious lesson and that hypocrisy is a sin to be punished.

In my opinion, the tone of this short farce is in sympathy with the "maerte." Despite the warning in the devil's epilogue, this short piece more equitably dramatizes the struggles of a "working girl," who tries to make a living justly, only to be treated unfairly, and discovers that she has no other course to follow.[105] She is insulted and humiliated by her mistress for trying to do her job as best she can. When she turns to "truancy," it is because earning an "honest living" has proven to be insufferable. Our sympathy is with her: her later escapades "truanting" with Brother Everaet are simply the necessary (and just?) compensations for her life of drudgery, misery and poverty. The "maerte" is excluded from the devil's epilogue precisely because she is in some respects "innocent," unlike her mentor, Brother Everaet.

Drie daghe here "Three days lord"

Drie daghe here is a fragment of which we have only the first 404 lines because one or more folios of the manuscript were lost. Leendertz has proposed that the farce is likely to have been as long as 780 lines, comparable in length therefore to the "abele spelen" and not the farces. This has led some critics to propose that *Drie daghe here* may have been a "burgerlijke" or urban "abel spel," although there is some reason to suspect that it is simply a farce, given the tone and scope of the piece and its similarity to the other farces in the collection.[106]

The play begins with a messenger who says he wants to present a good example of a shrewish wife. Then, for the next several lines, there is some confusion. The opening monologue spoken by Ghebuer ("neighbor man," later called "Imberecht") is disjointed (perhaps to simulate drunkenness?), with several asides to the audience, "these gawking fools" (v. 36). Ghebuer is then interrupted by an unspecified "wife" whom he seems not to notice. Once the play finally gets going we meet Jan, a drunk, who is married to a shrew named Bette. After much plotting, Jan bribes and convinces Bette to let him be master of his house for three days. She agrees—her reward, a fine fur pelt. Jan enjoys his new freedom, ordering his wife about, getting drunk, and bragging about his power. He invites Ghebuer and his wife, Lijsbeth, to supper that evening so he can show off. His neighbors arrive to find Bette somewhat tamed, receiving orders left and right from Jan. The climax comes when Ghebuer's wife tells Bette to use deceit and never to give up her power to get what she wants, because every woman is "made worse by what you've done" (v. 388). The farce leaves off with some suggestion that Ghebuer is going to try the same experiment at home with his wife. She, of course, doesn't think he'll be too successful. Had the play survived in its entirety, we probably would have followed the revenge of Bette on Jan when either three days or her patience had expired.

The Present Translation

This is the first complete English translation of the four "abele spelen" and the six farces contained in the Hulthem Manuscript. It is the first English translation, to my knowledge, of *Vanden Winter ende Vanden Somer, Die hexe, Drie daghe here,* and *Truwanten*. There are English translations of *Esmoreit* (Ayers, 1924; Oakshott and Streitmann, 1989), *Gloriant* (Judd, 1991), and *Lanseloet of Denemerken* (College, 1967; Geyl, 1924). *Rubben, Lippijn* and *De Buskenblaser* were recently translated into versions for performance before an English-speaking audience. I have added stage directions in parentheses for the benefit of the reader. Original rubrics are noted in the text.

In this translation I have tried to produce a language and a tone that replicate the original as accurately and sympathetically as possible. I wanted the elegance and the power of the original to come through. I have sacrificed the rhyming couplets of the original while seeking to reproduce the often lyric and nuanced rhythms of the Netherlandic text. I have also paid some attention to maintaining the integrity of each line (though it has not always been possible) so that a reader unfamiliar with Dutch could, with some effort, use the original in conjunction with the translation.

Some of the special problems of this text include the cumulative and repetitive forms of description that often divide a sentence or an idea into awkward and disjointed parts. For example, in Rogier's description of Florentijn to Gloriant, he says:

> This is Florentijn of Abelant,
> A noble and rich young lady.
> Her equal cannot be found in any pagan land.
> She is so excellent and her body so fair
> That on earth there are not five women who are
> The equal of my lady.
> She could not be more excellent,
> Cultivated, nor better formed.
> Her body is so perfect
> And her character so upright that
> There is no one born on earth
> Who is rich and high-born enough for her; no one
> Who has been able to gain her love,
> To make her his wife.
> She is a virgin, chaste and pure,
> And she has a father of great fame
> Who is, you know,
> The Red Lion of Abelant. (v. 262–79)

In this passage of eighteen lines the idea that Florentijn is "rich" is mentioned twice; that she is "excellent" is mentioned twice; that she has no equal is mentioned three times; that her body is "fair" is mentioned twice, and further, that she is noble, upright, and chaste, all somewhat repetitive of the general concept of her fitness and suitability for Gloriant as a wife. In the original text, these words are the same, and I have preserved much of this repetition for the cumulative if repetitive effect: Florentijn is quite perfect for Gloriant, except, as the last line warns, that her father is the Red Lion of Abelant, Gloriant's ancestral enemy. The repetition underscores how extraordinary Florentijn is and when the description stops, the impediment to her marrying Gloriant is revealed, even though Gloriant does not know it.

In a similar vein, descriptions are often awkwardly inserted into the middle of a sentence or an idea. For example, when Esmoreit wonders why his sister has not married, he says:

> O, Termagant and Apollo,
> That noble lady, my sister,
> Lives such a pure life,
> Why is it that she loves no man,
> Nor in all of the pagan land knows not one

> She'd like for a husband?
> By my God, Termagant,
> She has a noble nature.
> Perhaps she loves someone
> Secretly, someone about whom I know nothing
> Because she has never shown interest
> In any man alive.
> I wish Mohammed would give her a suitor
> Equal to her noble nature. (v. 405–18)

In this passage, the questions: "Why hasn't my sister married?" and "Perhaps she loves someone secretly?" (with the hope that Mohammed find her a worthy husband) are interrupted by idolizing and repetitive descriptions of Damiet. These descriptions of her serve not only to show us how excellent she is, but to reveal that Esmoreit, who is not really her brother, is fit to be her suitor because he already appreciates how excellent she is. Further, Esmoreit is concerned with her matrimonial status, a prelude to his desire to marry her himself as the scene unfolds. In all the plays, of which this is an example, the layered and repeated formulas usually, as in this case and the earlier example in *Gloriant*, point to another truth, often psychological or hidden, while the general direction of thought or argument or plot, as in this description of Damiet, seems to be leading elsewhere. In a simple example, Gheraert, Gloriant's uncle, tells Godevaert why Gloriant should marry:

> If he had a wife she would bear
> Children for the good of our country,
> This vast and great land,
> For it would truly be a shame if he died without an heir. (v. 46–9)

The awkwardly inserted line, "This vast and great land," and the two parallel but disjointed ideas, "If he had a wife she would bear children," and "It would truly be a shame if he died without an heir," again underscore the dilemma and at the same time deepen the sense of these lines. The country is foremost (Gloriant is after all its ruler) and as such it is underscored here: "She would bear children for the good of our country/ This vast and great land." For Gheraert it is the political implication of marriage that makes Gloriant's marriage so important: the country needs a confirmed line of succession. But instead, Gloriant maintains intensely personal, ultra-courtly, and even selfish reasons for not marrying: "I know no woman/ That I would make my wife" (v. 122–3), and "I myself know no woman of such high birth/ That I'd give even two pence for her" (v. 142–3). Gheraert concludes, "It would be a shame . . ." if Gloriant did not marry, "shame" as in the French "honte" —a deep and abiding shame with political and even spiritual implications.

NOTES

[1] W. van Androoij and A.M.J. van Buuren, in keeping with a general consensus, have recently shown that the manuscript was copied between 1399–1410. " 's Levens felheid in één band; het hanschrift-Van Hulthem," *Op belofte van profijt: Stadsliteratuur in de Nederlandse letterkunde der Middeleeuwen,* ed. H. Pleij (Amsterdam 1991), 189. H. Pleij, in keeping with recent arguments, suggests the middle of the fourteenth century for the date of composition, *De sneeuwpoppen van 1511. Stadscultuur in de late middeleeuwen* (Amsterdam 1988), 131, as do Jonckbloet, Leendertz, van Mierlo and Verdeyen. Some of the critics who would put these plays in the last quarter of the fourteenth century include Moltzer, Te Winkel, van der Riet, Endepols, and Ten Brink.

[2] A practice which is documented in Jan van Boedale's *Brabantsche Yeesten,* where a copyist is paid "drie nuwe stuvers" (three new nickles) for every thousand lines. The copyist protests, "Pro tali precio numquam plus scribere volo" (For that I'll never copy again) and dates his work 25 May 1444, *Truwanten* (1978), 11.

[3] P. Tack, "Onderzoek naar den ouderdom van het Hulthemse handschrift," *Het boek* 1 (1913), 81–91.

[4] W. van Androoij and A.M.J. van Buuren, " 's Levens felheid," 199.

[5] P. Leendertz, *Middelnederlandsche dramatische poëzie,* cxxxii–cxxxiii; J. van Mierlo, "Is Jan Dille de dichter van onze abele spelen?" *Verslagen en Mededelingen der Koninklijke Vlaamse Academie voor Taal- en Letterkunde* (1957); 77–8, 83; and G. Stuiveling, "De structuur van de abele spelen," *Vakwerk. Twaalf studies in literatuur* (1967), 33, 44.

[6] J.J. Gielen, *Belangrijke letterkunde werken. Leerdraad bij de studie der Nederlandse literatuur, deel I, Middeleeuwen en Vroeg-renaissance* (1932), 89.

[7] W. van Eeghem, "Jan Dille," *Brusselse Dichters.* Derde reeks (1958), 145–90. Van Mierlo, "Is Jan Dille de dichter van onze abele spelen?" *Verslagen en Mededelingen der Koninklijke Vlaamse Academie voor Taal- en Letterkunde* (1957), 7–8 and 83.

INTRODUCTION 51

[8] Van Mierlo thinks that a single author wrote these plays but not Jan Dille. He suggests that a poet from Brussels wrote them, perhaps for an acting company or a civic "kamer de rhetorica," *Schets eener Geschiedenis der Nederlansche letterkunde*, 2nd ed. (1950), 52.

[9] On the other hand, the designation may have been added by the scribe.

[10] See, for example, G. Stellinga (1954); Stuiveling (1967).

[11] In *Esmoreit*, Esmoreit overhears Damiet saying he's not her brother but an orphan prompting him to go in search of his family; in *Gloriant*, Floerant overhears Gloriant and Florentijn pledge their love to one another and goes to warn her father who imprisons them both; in *Lanseloet*, Lanseloet's mother overhears him courting Sanderijn prompting her to plot against their love; and in *Vanden Winter*, Moiaert, having listened to the entire argument between the seasons runs off to find Venus to save the day.

[12] G. Stellinga, *De abele spelen* (1995), 288–9.

[13] For a complete and excellent summary of the various and often contradictory views, see Roemans and van Assche, "Introduction," *Lanseloet van Denemerken*, 25–9.

[14] On the distinctions between the vernacular (vlaemsch) and the literary (dietsch), see Weevers, "The use of dietsch and duutsch, etc." and Weevers, *Poetry of the Netherlands* (London (1960), 14.

[15] J.A. Worp, *Geschiedenis van het drama* (1913), 82.

[16] P. Leendertz, *Middelnederlandsche dramatische poëzie* (1899–1907), cxxxii–cxxxiii.

[17] R. Verdeyen, *Beschouwingen* (1927), 537–45; see Roemans and van Assche for an excellent summary of many of these critical arguments, 21–24.

[18] P. Tack, "Onderzoek der ouderdom" (1913), 88–9; J.W. Muller, "Middelnederlandsche dramatische poëzie uitgegeven door P. Leendertz," *Museum* XVII (1910), 210–15.

[19] J. van Mierlo, "Een geestelijk lied uit de 13de eeuw," *Verslagen en Mededelingen der Koninklijke Vlaamsche Academie* (1941), 303–8.

[20] A. van Loey, "Esmoreitana," *Verslagen Mededelingen der Koninklijke Vlaamsche Academie* (1951), 83–6.

[21] W. van Androoij and A.M.J. van Buuren, " 's Levens felheid," 190–2.

[22] H. Pleij, "Hoe interpreteer je een middelnederlandse tekst?" *Spektator* 6 (1976–77), 346–9; *De sneeuwpoppen van 1511*, 131; L. Peters, "Esmoreit tconinx sone van Cecielien: Siciliaanse historie als abel spel," *Spiegel der Letteren* 19 (1977), 245–79.

[23] H.E. Moltzer, *Geschiedenis van het wereldlijk toneel in Nederland gedurende de Middeleeuwen* (1862), 37–72.

24 Jan te Winkel, *Geschiedenis van Nederlansche letterkunde* (1887), 514–5; Jan ten Brink, *Geschiedenis van Nedderlansche letterkunde* (1897), 217–8; Gerard Knuvelder, *Handboek tot de geschiedenis der Nederlandse letterkunde* (1970), 295; N.C.H. Wijngaards, "De oorsprong der abele spelen en sotternieën," *Handelingen der Koninklike Zuidernederlandse Maatschapij voor Taal- en Letterkunde en Geschiedenis* XXII (1968), 411–23.

25 J.A. Worp, *Geschiedenis van het drama* (1904), 92.

26 Stuiveling, *Schets van de Nederlandse letterkunde* (1966), 19.

27 See T. de Vroom, "*Renard* Retold: The Original *Van den Vos Reynaarde*," *Canadian Journal of Netherlandic Studies* VII.ii–IX.i (1987–88), 1–11.

28 While *Winter en Somer* is also called an "abel spel," in the rubrics, it is generically quite distinct from the other three plays because it is organized simply as a débat, ultimately a duel, between the two seasons.

29 For a thorough summary of the critical response to this term, see Roemans and van Assche, "De betekenis van abel," *Lanseloet van Denemerken* (1979), 8–15.

30 In this regard they are quite different in character from the *Miracles de Nostre Dame*, for example, in which Mary functions as the *dea ex machina* who turns the play's otherwise tragic outcome to comedy.

31 While *Vanden Winter* has no dramatic change in geographic setting, the entire structure of the play as a débat between winter and summer creates somewhat the same effect as great geographic shifts do.

32 On the subject of time and place in the plays, see G.A. van Es, "Het negeren van tijd en afstand in de abele spelen," *Tijdschrift voor Nederlandse Taal- en Letterkunde* 73 (1955), 161–92.

33 The two plays, *Esmoreit* and *The Winter's Tale*, share much the same story revolving around the calumnized wife who is forced to give up her child and imprisoned. Only when her child returns and "rescues" her, can reconciliation, understanding, forgiveness and ultimately, a marriage between the younger generation, take place. It is possible that Greene's *Pandosto*, one of the sources for Shakespeare's play, was influenced by a lost version of the Netherlandic play. For an outline of the similarities between the two, see Salingar, "Medieval stage heroines," *Shakespeare and the Traditions of Comedy* (1974), 47–53.

34 See W.J.A. Jonckbloet, *Geschiedenis der Nederlandsche letterkunde*, 3rd ed. (Gronningen: Wolters, 1885), II, 348–55 and J. te Wink, *De ontwikkelingsgang der Nederlandsche Letterkunde* (Harlem: Erven P. Bohn, 1922–27), II, 149–59.

35 Max Hermann, *Forschungen zur deutschen Theatergeschichte des Mittelalters und der Renaissance* (Berlin, 1914), 300–18.

INTRODUCTION 53

[36] Quoted and translated by Willem M.H. Hummelen, "Performers and Performance in the Earliest Secular Plays in the Netherlands," *Comparative Drama* 26 (1992), 22.
[37] Hummelen, 23.
[38] Hummelen, 19.
[39] Hummelen, 20.
[40] J. Beckers, "Van Hoofse toneeeltekst naar leestekst voor burgers? Enkele opmerkingen bij de Goudse druk van *Lanseloet*," *Literatuur* 6 (1989), 222–8. O.S.H. Lie, "Het abel spel van *Lanseloet van Denemerken* in het handschrift van Hulthem: hoofse tekst of stadsliteratuur," *Op de belofte van profijt*, ed. H. Pleij (1991), 200–16.
[41] H. van Dijk, " 'Als ons die astrominen lesen.' Over het abel spel *Vanden Winter ende vanden Somer*," *Tussentijds* (1985), 56–70.
[42] O.S.H. Lie, "Het abel spel van *Lanseloet*," 200–16.
[43] H. van Dijk, " 'Als ons die astrominen lesen.' " See the discussion on the play below.
[44] My translation of "de abele spelen, die z'on aangepast hoofse sfeer ademen, welke geheel op de maat lijkt gebracht van de zich emanciperende burgerij." H. Pleij, *De sneeuwpoppen van 1511* (Amsterdam, 1988), 131. The manuscript as a whole, however, presents a more interesting problem. Van Androoij and van Buuren have questioned the secular and profane cultural and historical context of this vast codex because it contains a large number of religious works. They suggest that the manuscript, taken as a whole, clearly has both secular and sacred aspects and that the civic or "burgerlijke" function should be examined in the context of the larger contents of the collection. van Androoij and van Buuren, 198.
[45] Leendertz, 2, lxxx.
[46] For a complete history of the printed editions of *Lanseloet*, see the chapter entitled "Tekstoverlevering" in Roemans and van Assche's *Lanseloet*, 53–70.
[47] Van der Riet, *Le Théâtre*, 127.
[48] For a discussion of the significance of these eighteenth-century scripts, see the facsimile and transcription by W.N.M. Hüsken and F.A.M. Schaars, *Sandrijn en Lanslot* (Nijmegen, 1985).
[49] H. van Dijk, "The drama texts in the Van Hulthem manuscript," *Medieval Dutch Literature in its European Context*, ed. E. Kooper (Cambridge, 1994), 289; E. van den Berg, *Middelnederlandse versbouw en syntaxis* (Utrecht, 1983), 188–223.
[50] L. Peters, "Esmoreit tconinx van Cecielien: Siciliaanse historie also abel spel," *Spiegel der Letteren* 19 (1977), 245–79; A.M. Duinhoven, "Introduction," *Esmoreit* (1979).

51 See Pleij and Peters for Fransiscan influences on these plays.
52 The Guelphs were particularly hated in the southern Netherlands and, therefore, Robbrecht would make a good villain for this audience who would happily see him hanged at the end of the play.
53 A.M. Duinhoven, "De bron van *Esmoreit*," *De nieuwe taalgids* 72 (1979), 124–44.
54 Comestor's *Historia* was a reworking and an expansion of the Vulgate on which Maerlant's rhymed text is based. Duinhoven (1979), 130.
55 J.B. Wolters, "Introduction," *Een abel spel van Esmoreit* (1960), 12.
56 R. Roemans and H. van Assche, eds. *Esmoreit* (1972), 43–57; "*Esmoreit* is wel het abel spel waarvoor het onderzoek naar een mogelijke bron het verst werd doorgevoerd," 43.
57 R. Preibsch, "Ein Beitrag zu den Quellen des Esmoreit," *Neophilologus* VII (1896), 241–3.
58 L. Salingar, "Medieval Stage Heroines," 47–52; C. Schlaugh, *Accused Queens*, 9–11, 53–9, 117–9.
59 Barabara L. Estrin, "The Foundling Plot: Stories in *The Winter's Tale*," *Modern Language Studies* 7 (1977), 27–38.
60 M. Ramondt, "De bronnen van Gloriant," *Tijdschrift for Nederlandse taal- en letterkunde* 61 (1922), 31–45.
61 The latter two were translated into Diets. Roemans and Gaspar, *Gloriant*, xxx–xxxi.
62 Leendertz, 2, clviii. "Esmeré" may be "Esmoreit."
63 The hertog of Bruyswyc is found in what was probably a Middle-Netherlandish work, the *Herzog von Brunenczwich*; in the German versions of the folksong about Henrek de Leeuw, the designation, *von Braunschweig*, is common; in Diets it is the *"Hertog van Bronswijk."* "Florentijn" may be a corrupt version taken from Apollonius of Tyre or from an edition of the *Gesta de septem Romanorum, Van de VII Vroeden van binnen Romen*. Roemans and Gaspar, xxxi.
64 Roemans and Gaspar, i; J. Notermans, 3.
65 *Wondervertelsels uit Vlaanderen*, ed. Pol de Mont and Alfons de Cock (1924), 190–5.
66 A.M. Duinhoven, " 'Gloriant' en 'Floris ende Blancefloer,' " *Tijdschrift voor taal- en letterkunde* 106, 2–3 (1990), 107–41.
67 Duinhoven, 113–4.
68 Duinhoven, 113–4.
69 Duinhoven, 138–9.
70 Lanseloet, however, is not very good at sticking to this position and instead sacrifices his good intentions to his desires by raping Sanderijn later in the play.

INTRODUCTION   55

71 For translated texts of Hadewijch and Beatrijs of Nazareth, see T. de Vroom, "Hadewijch Van Antwerpen (c.1250)," *Canadian Journal of Netherlandic Studies* IX.ii (Fall, 1990), 4–10; "Beatrijs of Nazareth," in *Women Writing in Dutch*, ed. Kristiaan Aercke (New York and London, 1994), 61–91.

72 Florentijn goes on to show that she is quite familiar with the details of the crucifixion and death of Christ (v. 1034–46).

73 It is unclear in just what capacity Sanderijn serves Lanseloet's mother; she may be a lady-in-waiting and therefore of a much higher class than a simple serving girl. Later in the play, when "The Knight," her future husband, asks Sanderijn about her parentage, he is pleased to hear that she was born "from a noble family" (v. 467). In this case, it may be that Lanseloet's mother is the one who exaggerates Sanderijn's low birth as an impediment to the marriage.

74 P. Leendertz, *Middelnederlandsche dramatische poëzie*, 13–4.

75 G. Kazemier, "Lanseloet van Denemerken," *Taal- en letterkundig gastenboek voor Prof. G.A. van Es. Opstellen, de 70-jarige aangeboden ter gelegenheid van zijn afscheid als hoogleraar aan de Rijksuniversiteit te Groningen* (Groningen, 1975), 229–35.

76 There are actually two "servant girls," women of lower station, whom Duinhoven cites as versions of Sanderijn. A.M. Duinhoven, "De bron van Lanseloet," *Tijdschrift voor Nederlandse taal- en letterkunde* 95 (1979), 262–87.

77 G. Kazemier, "De bron van Lanseloet?" *Tijdschrift voor Nederlandse taal- en letterkunde* 96 (1980), 1–11. For an interesting exchange and rebuttal, see Duinhoven's response and Kazemier's rejoinder in the same issue, 12–18.

78 Lanseloet's sentiment mirrors Gloriant's earlier and indeed may have the same source. According to Lie, the treatise' popularity is born out by the number of surviving manuscripts, five in total from the end of the fourteenth and the beginning of the fifteenth century. O.S.H. Lie, "Het abel spel van *Lanseloet*" (1991).

79 *Vander feesten een proper dinc*, ed. Werkgroep van Groningse neerlandci, 1972.

80 While the stage direction "Now she has been with him in the room," is not explicit, it is clear from the textual evidence in Sanderijn's speech later that she has been raped. As Jeanette Koekmann has pointed out, it is startling how many critics have argued that Sanderijn was not raped but seduced by Lanseloet—or how many critics aren't sure whether she was raped! Koekmann shows that there is ample evidence Sanderijn was raped particularly in her soliloquy after the event which clearly points to the "knowledge" (324–5) that she's been violated and

further, that it was done against her will (342–4). "De stilte rond Sanderijn: over het abel spel *Lanseloet van Denemerken*," *De canon onder vuur. Nederlandse literatuur tegendraads gelezen*, ed. E. van Alphen and M. Meijer (1991), 20–34. See also Roemans and van Assche, "Verleiding of verkrachting?" *Lanseloet van Danemerken*, 49–50.

[81] For a comparison between Lanseloet's dishonorable actions and their revision by this knight, see Lie, "Het abel spel van *Lanseloet*" (1991).

[82] Roemans and van Assche, 44. My translation. Both van Mierlo and the Norwegian scholar of Dutch literature, K. Langvik-Johannessen, also agree that *Lanseloet* is a tragedy for the same reasons. For a discussion of these views, see H. van Dijk, "*Lanseloet van Denemerken*," *Popular Drama in Northern Europe in the Later Middle Ages*, ed., Fleming G. Andersen, Julia McGrew, Tom Pettitt, and Reinholdt Schröder (Odense, 1986), 111–2.

[83] O.S.H. Lie, "Het abel spel van *Lanseloet*," 207.

[84] N.C.H. Wijngaards, "Structuurvergelijking bij de abele spelen," *Levende Taalen* 43 (1962), 326.

[85] K. Iwema, "De wereld van een abel spel, *Vanden winter ende vanden somer*, herbescowd," *De nieuwe taalgids* 80 (1987), 21–7.

[86] H. van Dijk, "'Als ons die astrominen lesen,'" 56–70. K. van de Waerden, "Harmonisatie van het wereld beeld. Het abel spel *Vanden winter ende vanden somer*," *Forum der Letteren* 35 (1994), 94–109.

[87] K. Iwema, "De wereld van een abel spel," 21–7. See also H. Walther, *Das streitgedicht in der lateinschen literatur des Mittelalters* (München, 1920).

[88] D. van der Poel, "De rol van Venus in *Vanden winter ende vanden somer*," *In de zevende hemel* (Groningen, 1935), 185–9.

[89] *Rubben, Lippijn, De Buskenblaser*, and *Drie Daghe Here* clearly address this question; *Die Hexe* and *Truwanten* do not.

[90] For a discussion of the figure of the cuckold in the play, see A.M. Duinhoven's preface to the text of the farce, "De sotternie van *Lippijn*," *Klein Kapitaal uit het handschrift — Van Hulthem* (Hilversum, 1992), 122–3.

[91] My translation of: "Opgemerkt dient te worden dat de duivel is als een goochelaar die, omdar hij alle omstanders bij zijn vorstelling wil uitnodigen tot lachen, in een doosje blaast, waarin vuiligheid zit, en in geen enkel opzicht blijkt hij bezoedeld; toen hij het doosje had aangereikt aan meer mensen, bleken die daardoor niet bezoedeld, nadat ze in het doosje geblazen hadden. Tenslotte gaf hij het doosje aan een domoor om erin te blazen, hem die kant toedraaiend waar de vuiligheid was, en toen hij blies kwam uit dat busje plotseling pikzwarte stof, zijn gehele gelaat zwartmakend en bezoedelend; door zijn verwarring en bezoedeling werden alle omstanders van de voorstelling tot lachen

en applaus gebracht. Zo draait de duivel, als een dwaas in het verborgene wil zondigen, hem als het ware het doosje van bezoedeling toe." Quoted in: "Die Buskenblaser," ed. H. van Dijk, F. Kramer, and J. Tersteg, *Klein Kapitaal*, 164.

92 H. Pleij, "De sociale funktie van humor en trivialiteit op het rederijkerstoneel," *Spektator* 5 (1975–76), 121.

93 They point especially to the repeated use of "I can" in the monologue, characteristic of this genre. Van Dijk, Kramer and Tersteg, 166. A.M. Duinhoven has suggested that there are textual problems in the first monologue and scene and that some lines spoken by the "one man," are really spoken by the "second man," and vice versa, "Boerenbedrog in Die Buskenblaser," *De nieuwe taalgids* 87 (1994), 195–203.

94 Really a "knecht," for which "servant" is the equivalent English word, though "knecht" implies more the workman, mender, handyman which "the first man" proposes himself to be at the start of the farce.

95 H. van Dijk, Kramer and Tersteg, 167; see also A.G. Stewart, *Unequal Lovers. A Study of Unequal Couples in Northern Art* (New York, 1977), 18.

96 H. van Dijk, Kramer and Tersteg, 168.

97 "Doosje," like "busken," is literally a little box but it is also an obscene reference to a woman's genitals. *Woordenboek des Nederlandsche Taal* (4) ed. J.A.N. Knuttel (1908), vol. III.2.

98 J. Vromans, "Die Hexe," *Klein Kapitaal*, 181–9.

99 With a pun on "lullen": 1) to pray/mumble/sing; 2) to seduce by talking; 3) to have sex with.

100 Quoted in *Truwanten* (1978), 95. Much of what follows is taken from an essay in this excellent edition of the play called "Cultuurhistorische achtergronden," *Werkgroep van Brusselse en Utrechtse nederlandici*, 1978.

101 "Souvenirs" of this sort might include a small cloth with the head of Christ painted on it in imitation of Veronica's napkin to indicate that the wearer had been to Jerusalem and seen the original; or a scallop shell, to indicate that he or she had visited Santiago de Compostella. The "pilgrim" had a built-in disguise, like a cleric, a costume to make him or her recognizable to others, and yet, as in this case, to deceive others further.

102 R.E. Lerner, "Vagabonds and Little Women: The Medieval Netherlandish Dramatic Fragment 'De truwanten,' " *Modern Philology* 65 (1967), 301–7.

103 H. Pleij, "De sociale functie ... ," 108–27.

104 *Truwanten*, 101, 105, 111.

[105] For the lack of suitable work and living conditions for a young, unmarried girl in fourteenth-century Netherlands, see *Truwanten*, 93.
[106] Leendertz, 2: cxviii–cxx; Stellinga, "Uitleiding," *Vanden Winter*, 96–7.

BIBLIOGRAPHY

Editions of the Plays

Older Editions

Hoffman von Fallersleben, H., ed. *Altniederländische Schaubühne. Abele Spelen ende Sotternien herausgegeben von etc.* Horae Belgicae VI, 1838.

Moltzer, H.E. *De Middelnerderlandsche dramatische poëzie.* Groningen, 1868–75.

Leendertz, P. *Middelnederlandsche dramatische poëzie.* 2 vols. Leiden, 1899–1907. This edition is still very important because of its excellent notes and commentary.

Recent Collected Editions

van Kammen, L., ed. *De Abele Spelen, naar het Hulthemse handschrift.* Amsterdam, 1969. Edition in Middle Dutch of the plays and their four accompanying farces.

Komrij, G., ed. and trans. *De Abele spelen.* The Hague, 1989. Middle Dutch and Modern Dutch, facing pages, this edition contains all four "abele spelen," and the four sotties which accompany them in a rhyming, verse translation which is very readable.

Middeleeuws toneel: Esmoreit, Gloriant, Lanseloet van Denemerken, Nu Noch, Elckerlijc, Mariken van Nieumeghen. Utrecht and Antwerp, 1984.

Duinhoven, A.M. ed. *Klein kapitaal uit het handschrift van Hulthem.* Hilversum, 1992, 122–38.

Esmoreit

Duinhoven, A.M., ed. *Esmoreit.* Zutphen, 1975.

Notermans, R. and R. Gaspar, eds. *Een abel spel van Esmoreit.* Zwolle, 1955.

Roemans, R. and R. Gaspar, eds. *Een abel spel van Esmoreit.* Klassieke Galerij, no. 98. Antwerpen, 1954.

Verdeyen, R. and C.G. Kaakebeen, eds. *Esmoreit: abel spel uit de veertiende eeuw.* 17th ed. Groningen, 1960.

Gloriant

Notermans, J., ed. *Een abel spel ende een edel dinc vanden hertoghe van Bruuyswijc, Gloriant.* Batavia and Groningen, 1948.

Roemans, R. and R. Gaspar, eds. *Gloriant.* Klassieke Galerij, no. 102. Amsterdam and Antwerp, 1956; 1970.

Stellinga, G., ed. *Gloriant van Bruuyswijc.* Culemborg, 1976.

Lanseloet of Denmark

Roemans, R. and H. van Assche, eds. *Lanseloet van Denemerken.* 8th ed. Antwerp, 1982.

Stellinga, G., ed. *Lanseloet van Denemerken.* Gorinchem, 2nd ed. 1975.

Hier beghint een seer ghenoechlike ende amoroeze historie vanden eedelen Lantsloet ende die scone Sanderijn. 's-Gravenhage, 1920. Facsimile edition of the Goudse incunabulum published by the printer, Govert van Ghemen, between 1486 and 1492.

Hüsken, W.N.M. and F.A.M. Schaars. *Sandrijn en Lanslot.* Diplomatische uitgave van twee toneelrollen uit het voormalig archief van de Rederijkerskamer De Fiolieren te 's- Gravenpolder. Nijmegen, 1985. Facsimile and diplomatic edition of two actors' scripts from the Dutch province of Zeeland dating from 1720.

Vanden Winter ende vanden Somer

Antonissen, R., ed. *Een abel spel Vanden Winter ende Vanden Somer naar het Hulthemsche Handschrift uitgegeven.* Klassieke Galerij, no. 6. Antwerpen, 1946.

Stellinga, G., ed. *Het Abel Spel Vanden Winter ende Vanden Somer ende ene Sotternie, Rubben.* Zutphen, 1963.

The Farces

Vijf Sotternieen: Tekts en Vertaling (Lippijn, De Buskenblaser, Die Hexe, Rubben, Nu Noch). Ed. and trans. into modern Dutch by H. Adema. Leeuwarden, 1985.

"De Buskenblaser," *"Gloriant" gevolgd door "De Buskenblaser".* Ed. G. Stellinga. Culemborg, 1976, 96–111.

"Die Buskenblaser," *Klein kapitaal uit het handschrift van Hulthem,* ed. H. van Dijk, F. Kramer, and J. Tersteg. Hilversum, 1992, 122–138.

"Die hexe," *Klein kapitaal uit het handschrift van Hulthem,* ed. J. Vromans, Hilversum, 1992, 180–9.

"Lippijn," *Klein kapitaal uit het handschrift van Hulthem,* ed. A.M. Duinhoven. Hilversum, 1992, 122–38.

"Drie daghe here," *Het Abel Spel Vanden Winter ende Vanden Somer.* 2nd ed. Ed. G. Stellinga. Zutphen, 1975, 7–30.

"Rubben," *Het abel spel Vanden Winter ende Vanden Somer.* 2nd ed. Ed. G. Stellinga. Zutphen, 1963, 72–86.

"*Truwanten*," *Het Abel Spel Vanden Winter ende Vanden Somer*. 2nd ed. Ed. G. Stellinga. Zutphen, 1963, 31–7.

Truwanten. Ed., trans. into modern Dutch, and commentary by the Werkgroep van Brusselse en Utrechtse neerlandici. *De nieuwe taalgids cahiers* no. 6. Groningen, 1978.

English Translations

Ayres, H.M. *An Ingenious Play of Esmoreit*. Introd. Adriaan J. Barnouw. The Hague, 1924. An edition in rhyming couplets, which, according to Barnouw, tries to accurately represent "the poetical flavor of the old Dutch verse" (xxxi).

Beidler, P. and Therese Decker. "*Lippijn*," *Chaucer Review* 23 (1989) 237–42.

College, E. "*Lancelot of Denmark*," *Reynard the Fox and Other Mediaeval Netherlands Secular Literature*. London and New York, 1967. 165–183. A prose translation.

Decker, T. and M. Walsh. "Three Sotternien: Farcical Afterpieces from the Hulthem Manuscript." *Dutch Crossing* (Autumn, 1992), 73–96. Includes translations of "*Lippijn*," "*De Buskenblaser*," and "*Rubben*," a rhyming verse translation which "tries to follow the literal translation as closely as possible and yet create a dramatic text suitable for playing."

Geyl, P. *Lancelot of Denmark. A Beautiful Play*. The Hague, 1924.

Judd, S., "*Gloriant*," Introd. T.M. Guest. *Dutch Crossing* 43 (Spring, 1991) 70–93.

Oakshott, J. and E. Streitmann. *An Excellent Play of Esmoreit, Prince of Sicily*. Lancaster, England, 1989. A rhyming verse translation designed for production, rpt. with alterations of "*An Excellent Play of Esmoreit, Prince of Sicily*," *Dutch Crossing* 30 (Fall, 1986), 3–39.

Other Works

van Androoij, W. and A.M.J. van Buuren, " 's Levens felheid in een band: Het handschrift—van Hulthem," *Op belofte van profijt. Stadsliteratuur in de Nederlandse letterkunde der Middeleeuwen*, ed. H. Pleij. Amsterdam, 1991.

College, E., ed. *Reynard the Fox and Other Netherlands Secular Literature*, trans. A. Barnouw and E. College. London and New York, 1967.

Decker, T. "*Lanseloet van Denemerken* and its Biblical Source," *Canadian Journal of Netherlandic Studies* 8.2–9.1 (Fall, 1987–Spring 1988), 12–27.

Delepierre, O. *A Sketch of the History of Flemish Literature and its Celebrated Authors*. New York, 1973; rpt. of 1860.

van Dijk, H. "'Als ons die astrominen lesen.' Over het abel spel *Vanden winter ende vanden somer.*" *Tussentijds* [festschrift W.P. Gerritsen], ed. A.M.J. van Buuren. Utrecht, 1985, 56–70.

——. "*Lanseloet van Denemerken*, One of the Abele Spelen in the Hulthem Manuscript," *Popular Drama in Northern Europe in the Later Middle Ages: A Symposium*, ed. Fleming G. Andersen, Julia McGrew, Tom Pettitt, and Reinhold Schröder. Odense, 1986, 101–12.

——. "The drama texts in the Van Hulthem manuscript," *Medieval Dutch Literature in its European Context*, ed. E. Kooper. *Cambridge Studies in Medieval Literature* 21, 1994, 283–96.

van Dijk, H., W. Hummelen, W. Hüsken, and E. Streitmann. "A Survey of Dutch Drama Before the Renaissance," *Dutch Crossing* 22 (1984), 35–58.

——. "The Structure of the 'sotternieën' in the Hulthem Manuscript," *Theatre in the Middle Ages*. Mediaevalia Lovaniensia Series I, Studia XIII. Leuven, 1985, 238–50.

Duinhoven, A.M. "De bron van Esmoreit," *De nieuwe taalgids* 72 (1979), 124–44.

——. "De bron van Lanseloet," *Tijdschrift voor Nederlandse taal- en letterkunde* 72 (1979), 262–87.

——. "*Gloriant* en *Floris ende Blanchefloer*," *Tijdschrift voor Nederlandse taal- en letterkunde* 106, no. 2–3 (1990), 107–41.

Endepols, H.J.E. *Het decoratief en de opvoering van het Middelnederlandsche drama volgens de Middelnederlandsche tooneelstucken*. Amsterdam, 1903.

Enklaar, D.Th. "Een illustratie van het abel spel van Lanseloet," *Lezende in Buurmans Hof: Literair-Historische Opstellen*. Zwolle, 1956, 52–4.

Gossens, J. "De iconographie door Lanseloet van Denemerken," *Handelingen van de Koninklijke Zuidnederlandse Maatschappij voor Taal- en Letterkunde en Geschiedenis* 30 (1976), 73–88.

Hollar, J.M. and E.W.F. van den Elzen. "Toneelleven in Deventer in de vijftiende en zestiende eeuwe," *De nieuwe taalgids* 73–5 (1980), 412–25.

Hummelen, W.M.H. "Tekst en toneelrichting in de abele spelen," *De nieuwe taalgids* 70 (1977), 229–42.

——. "Performers and Performance in the Earliest Secular Plays in the Netherlands," *Comparative Drama* 26 (1992–93), 19–33.

Hunningher, B. "The Netherlandish Abele Spelen," *Maske und Kothurn* 10 (1964), 244–53.

Iwema, K. "De wereld van een abel spel. *Vanden winter ende vanden somer* herbeschouwd," *De nieuwe taalgids* 80 (1987), 21–7.

——. "Waer sidi—over een middelnederlandse toneelconventie," *De Nieuwe Taalgids* 77 (1984), 48–61.

Koekmann, J. "De stilte rond Sanderijn; over het abel spel *Lanseloet van Denemerken,*" *De canon onder vuur. Nederlandse literatuur tegendraads gelezen,* ed. E. van Alphen and M.N. Meijer. Amsterdam, 1991.

Lie, O.S.H. "Het abel spel van *Lanseloet van Denemerken* in het handschrift van Hulthem: hoofse tekst of stadsliteratuur?" *Op belofte van profijt. Stadsliteratuur in de Nederlandse letterkunde van de Middeleeuwen,* ed. H. Pleij. Amsterdam, 1991.

Meredith, P. and J.E. Taily, eds. *The Staging of Religious Drama in the Later Middle Ages: Texts and Documents in English Translation.* Kalamazoo, Michigan, 1983.

Moltzer, H.E. *Geschiedenis van het wereldlijk tooneel in Nederland gedurende de Middeleeuwen.* Leiden, 1862.

Notermans, J. "Mohammedaanse elementen in twee abele spelen: *Esmoreit* en *Gloriant,*" *Belgisch Tijdschrift voor Filologie en Geschiedenis* 51 (1973), 624–42.

van Oostrom, F. *Aanvaard dit werk: Over Middelnederlandse auteurs en hun publiek.* Amsterdam, 1992.

Pleij, H. "De sociale functie van humor en trivialiteit op het rederijkerstoneel," *Spektator* 5 (1975–76), 108–27.

———. "Hoe interpreteer je een Middelnederlandse tekst?" *Spektator* 6 (1976–77), 337–49.

———. *Het literaire leven in de Middeleeuwen.* Leiden, 1984.

———. *De sneeuwpoppen van 1511. Standscultuur in de late Middeleeuwen.* Amsterdam, 1988.

Pleij, H., ed. *Op de belofte van profijt. Stadsliteratuur in de Nederlandse letterkunde der Middeleeuwen.* Amsterdam, 1991.

———. "Volkfeest en toneel in de middeleeuwen." *De Revisor* 3 (1976), 52–63.

van der Riet, F. J. *Théatre Profane Sérieux en Langue Flamande Au Moyen Âge.* The Hague, 1936.

Salingar, L. "Medieval Stage Romances," *Shakespeare and the Traditions of Comedy.* Cambridge, 1974.

Schlaugh, M. *Chaucer's Constance and Accused Queens.* New York, 1927.

Stellinga, G. *Zinsvormen en zinsfuncties in de abele spelen.* Groningen and Djakarta, 1954.

Streitman, E. "The Low Countries," *The Theatre of Medieval Europe: New Research in Early Drama,* ed. E. Simon. Cambridge, 1991, 225–52.

Stuiveling, G. "De structuur van de abele spelen," *Vakwerk: Twaalf studies in literatuur.* Zwolle, 1967.

Tack, P. "Onderzoek naar den ouderdom van het Hulthemese handschrift." *Het boek* 2 (1913), 81–91.

Traver, H. "Religious Implications in the Abele Spelen of the Hulthem Manuscript," *Germanic Review* 26 (1951), 34–49.

Verdam, J. and F. Verwijs. *Middelnederlandsch Handwoordenboek.* 2 vols. s'Gravenhage, 1885–1981.

Waerden, K. van de. "Harmonisatie van het wereldbeeld. Het abel spel *Vanden Winter ende vanden Somer* in cultuurfilosofisch perspectief," *Forum der Letteren* 35 (1994), 95–109.

Weevers, T. "The Medieval Drama in the Netherlands." *Poetry of the Netherlands in its European Context 1170–1930.* London, 1960.

———. "The use of dietsch and duutsch, etc.," *London Medieval Studies* 1 (1939).

Worp, J.A. *Geschiedenis van het drama en van het tooneel in Nederland.* Part I. Groningen, 1904.

"Van den Hertog van Brunswijk," *Wondervertelsels uit Vlaanderen,* ed. and transcribed by Pol de Mont and Alfons de Cock. Zutphen, 1924, 190–5.

Netherlandic Secular Plays

The "Abele Spelen"
and
the Farces
of the Hulthem Manuscript

P. Bruegel, *The Calumny of Apelles*. London, British Museum.

ESMOREIT

The Abel Spel of Esmoreit
the son of the King of Sicily,
and the farce which follows it.

Dramatis Personae

The KING of Sicily
The QUEEN of Sicily
ESMOREIT, son of the King of Sicily
ROBBRECHT, cousin of Esmoreit
The KING of Damascus
PLATUS, fortune teller and astrologer to the King
    of Damascus, sometimes called, "Meester"
DAMIET, the daughter of the King of Damascus

PROLOGUE

> God, who was born of the Virgin,
> Did not want destroyed
> That which he had made with his own hands,
> So he promised to die naked as he was born
> In complete fidelity, his death for our debt.
> Now I ask you, lords and ladies,
> Be quiet and you shall hear:
> How there once was a king
> Who ruled Sicily,
> Whose wife bore him a son   10
> (listen, and you shall learn marvelous things).

At his court there was a villain
Named Robbrecht, his brother's son,
Who had the right to rule,
Who would have taken the crown
If the king had died without an heir.
But then a little prince was born,
And Robbrecht's loss was bitter,
He bore the child a heart of stone.
Now in a little while you shall hear   20
What happened to this boy:
How Robbrecht made him suffer;
How he sold him to a Saracen,
And delivered him up to despair.
You shall hear how the mother who bore him
Was imprisoned where she
Would never see the moon or sun,
How she did not smile for twenty years.
Robbrecht was the cause of all her sorrows.
Now be still and mark how it begins.   30

[*In Sicily*]

ROBBRECHT [*alone*]: God's curse, the time has come
For the long-awaited birth
Of my sometime cousin, Esmoreit!
I would have been king
When my uncle dropped dead,
But now the old geezer and his wife
Have gotten a child!
O Sicily, richest of gardens!
Noble forest, greatest of kingdoms!
Will I live in this paradise   40
Only to be your bastard?[1]
My heart is heavy!
By the God who made me,
I shall plot day and night
To ruin that child even if

It costs me my life! Let me see,
(indeed, I shall plot day and night),
To smother him! To drown him!
Even if pain should come to my door,
I myself will be the king 50
Of this great land Sicily!
And I'll get her too, I'll drag her down,
The queen, my uncle's wife,
So that noble lord, my uncle, will never again
Share his body with her.
And then, if in these things I do succeed,
The country will be mine.

[*In Damascus*]

PLATUS: Where are you your highness,
Great lord of Damascus?
My heart is full of anguish 60
Remembering things I have seen. . . .
KING [*entering*]: Meester Platus, what have you seen
That makes you so forlorn?
PLATUS: Lord King, last night toward morning
I was outside in a field
When I saw the heavens fixed,
The planets in the firmament were
                            configured and
Foretelling that in Christendom a child
Is born of high degree
Who one day will kill you with his sword. 70
He will take your life, Lord King,
And your daughter will be his wife
And she will become a Christian.
KING: Meester, tell me
When was this child born?
PLATUS: The young one was born last night,
Lord King, since you ask, and
In the Christian land of Sicily

	His father is a great king.	
KING:	Meester, let me understand,	80
	Is this really what will happen?	
PLATUS:	Yes, Lord King, by Apollo,	
	Unless you meet it with the might to prevent it.
	If you want to act wisely	
	I shall advise you	
	How and in what manner	
	You may keep your state,	
	For good, sound advice	
	Is called for in this matter.	
KING:	I am astonished by	90
	The things you tell me,	
	My heart is so perplexed that	
	I cannot imagine what to do!	
	You are a wise man,	
	Platus, counselor, dear friend,	
	You have served me loyally and for many years
	And you have often given me	
	the wise counsel which
	Protected my honor and my estate.
	Now I pray you, counselor, trusted and good,
	That without delay	100
	You help find a way	
	For me to keep my state	
	And not be vanquished by this young child,
	The one that you have told me so much about.
	Tell me how I can escape his might.
PLATUS:	Lord King, noble baron, and	
	Noblest of heroes, hear me now:	
	Without delay, give me	
	A treasure to take with me	
	And immediately I will	110
	Ride to Sicily.	
	There I will use all my skill to get
	The young high-born lord.	

ESMOREIT

	I pray Mohammed to help me:	
	Let my plans take root,	
	For I shall not return until	
	I can bring him to your kingdom.	
	Therefore, give me silver and gold.	
	I will steal him or buy him,	
	Or get him with cunning	120
	—Already, I can guess what to do—	
	And then he will be yours.	
	We will teach him according to our law and	
	He will become a good pagan	
	Because he will think that you are his father,	
	And so you will be saved.	
	Now quickly, it's time,	
	I will travel with speed.	
KING:	Platus, my counselor, this advice is sound.	
	Go hence and haste your journey;	130
	I want you to spare nothing.	
	Take enough treasure in your possession	
	And don't waste time counting it out.	
	Bring me the young one,	
	This I pray above all things,	
	To this end spare no cost,	
	For I have a great desire	
	To see this young man.	
PLATUS:	Lord King, I am your loyal servant,	
	I shall think of nothing else day and night.	140

[*Back in Sicily sometime later*]

ROBBRECHT	[*alone*]: I have waited a long time
	But finally I 've gotten what I wanted!
	I have the young one, the one who is so prized
	By my uncle, the old gray one,
	And by his mother. They think
	There's never been a more beautiful child!
	He makes me sick! The time has come

| | For me to deprive them of their joy.
| | [*speaking to the child*] You must be vanquished
| | And so too those who brought you to life.   150
| | Esmoreit, you must die,
| | It must be so, and it will drive them mad!
| | I will drown you in a well.
| | Or kill you in a crueler way!
| | For because of your birth, I cannot rest,
| | Day and night, there is no joy in my heart.
| PLATUS | [*overhearing him*]: O friend, that would be terrible,
| | He is such a beautiful child.
| | You must be mad
| | To want to kill this young prince.   160
| | I see by your anger that you are resolute,
| | Your tirade makes that clear.
| | But I pray you, tell me what has happened that
| | You are so against him?
| ROBBRECHT: | Friend, when he was born of his mother
| | And entered into the world
| | It came to me in a dream
| | That one day this child would take my life.
| | Since that time I have become so anxious
| | That I couldn't rest, I couldn't endure the fear.   170
| | So I waited hour after hour
| | And finally I stole him from his mother.
| | Before he escapes me
| | I mean to put him to death.
| PLATUS: | Friend, I have a better idea,
| | Listen to me.
| | [*Looking at the child*] By Apollo I ask you,
| | When was he born?
| | He is clearly of high birth.
| | I will buy him from you at once   180
| | And take him with me from this country
| | To the land of the pagans; do you know
| | The state of Balderijs

ESMOREIT

	Which lies past Turkey?[2]	
ROBBRECHT:	Friend, if you want to buy this young boy	
	I will tell you	
	Who bore him and who conceived him	
	I will tell you all:	
	The King of Sicily is his father,	
	A high-born hero,	190
	And his mother, you must hear all,	
	Is the daughter of the King of Hungary.	
PLATUS:	Friend, is he of such high born parents?	
	That explains why the young one likes me.	
	I will buy him, if you will.	
	Now speak up, how much do you want for him?	
ROBBRECHT:	Friend, you can have him	
	For a neat thousand pounds of gold.	
PLATUS:	All right friend, there's your money,	
	Now give me the young boy.	200
	But tell me one thing,	
	Tell me, what is his name?	
ROBBRECHT:	Esmoreit is what they call the young lord,	
	Esmoreit is his name.	
PLATUS:	He will become a pagan,	
	Of this you can be certain.	
	Now Mohammed, protect me,	
	For I must travel far with my charge.	
	[PLATUS *exits with child*]	
ROBBRECHT	[*alone*]: Now my heart is unburdened,	
	The great pain I have born is gone,	210
	He'll be lost forever in a pagan land,	
	Of this I am certain because	
	The state of Balderijs	
	Lies past Turkey in a far off place.	
	God make him suffer for	
	He has perplexed my heart!	
	Now I will go and secretly put this money	

	In a safe place.
	It is sovereign gold.
	And if the kingdom is denied me 220
	Well then I'll still be a rich lord
	With all the gold I have gotten for him.
	Never mind — I have carried out my plans —
	And I am certain that the kingdom will
	one day be mine.

[*Later in Damascus,* PLATUS *returning with the child*]

PLATUS: Where are you, your highness,
Great lord of Damascus?
Now come and see the young boy
Who was born of noble blood.

KING: [*entering*]: Nothing has ever made me so happy
As this gift. 230
I will raise him as my child,
I will put him in my daughter's care.

PLATUS: All well and good, Lord King,
                but you must hide
Everything else from your daughter:
You must not tell her
Who his mother and father are
Because grief will ultimately
Come from it,
For in their hearts, women are weak.
If you tell her of his high birth 240
Then mighty Venus will
Make her love the young boy, and then
She will have to tell him
How it is that he came here.
For, Lord King, the fire of love
Will spring up in your daughter
When he comes of age.
Therefore don't tell her a thing
Other than that he's a foundling —

	The less you tell her, the better.	250
KING:	Platus, Platus, by Termagant,	
	What you're telling me makes sense.	
	Let's keep this business secret	
	From my daughter forever,	
	Only then will I be at peace.	

[*turning to look for his daughter*]

	Where are you, daughter, Damiet?	
	Come to me at once,	
	I must speak with you, by Mohammed.	

[*Enter* DAMIET]

DAMIET:	Father, I am at your service with pleasure.	
	Tell me, what is your wish?	260
KING:	Damiet, by my god,	
	Look here at the ruby lips	
	Of this young foundling boy, who	
	Mohammed has given to me.	
	I heard him crying	
	When I was walking in the orchard.	
	I found this young one there	
	Under a cedar tree.	
	Damiet, take care of him	
	And treat him like your brother;	270
	You must be his sister and his mother.	
	The young man's name is Esmoreit.	
DAMIET:	Father, Lord, by Termagant,	
	I never saw a more beautiful child.	
	For what Mohammed has sent us,	
	I thank him and Apollo too.	
	I will gladly be his sister and his mother.	

[*Exit* KING *and* PLATUS; DAMIET *and the young boy remain*]

	O dearest little child,	
	You are the most beautiful thing	
	My eyes have ever seen.	280

I am right to thank Mohammed
That I have a brother;
I will gladly be your sister and mother.
O Esmoreit, beautiful child,
. How it amazes me
That you were found without guard,
For judging from the swaddling clothes
                                    you wear,
It seems to me that you are descended
                            from noble blood.
Now come with me, beautiful little boy,
I will treat you as my brother.   290

[*Meanwhile, in Sicily*]

KING: Where are you, Robbrecht, my dear cousin?
Come to me, I must speak with you.
I think my heart will break
I am so tormented with sorrow.

ROBBRECHT [*entering*]: O Uncle, noblest of men,
Why are you so upset?

KING: Grief has put me so low
That I think my heart will break.
I have lost my beautiful child,
My son, Esmoreit,   300
I could not be more sad about it.
If in the same instant I had lost
My wealth and my kingdom too
I would weep less than for this,
The loss of my beautiful child.
O me, O me, the bitter sorrow
That I and my wife now suffer.
I think it will cost me my life.
And my wife, that noble woman,
Her heart is in despair.   310
I'd rather be dead
Than to live in this torment.

ROBBRECHT:	O Noble Uncle of great renown,
	Do not weep like this
	Because I know how it happened!
	Even though my aunt seems to suffer
	I am certain
	She does not feel real torment.
	Her heart is full of hate toward you
	Because you are old in your days. 320
	I have frequently heard her complain,
	When she didn't know I could hear.
	I think she still plots,
	Lord king, uncle, to take your life.
	She will try to poison you,
	Of that I am certain,
	For I have heard her speak so cruelly
	When I stood listening in secret
	But I didn't say a word
	Until this moment. 330
	I am certain that she herself
	Brought the child to his death
	Because she could never stand you,
	You with your gray beard.
	She is looking for something more,
	Surely she loves a younger man.
KING:	By the father who made me,
	Cousin Robbrecht I know that
	Neither money nor prayer can help her now,
	I will kill her, that cruel wife of mine. 340
ROBBRECHT:	Uncle, I bet my life on it,
	What I've told you is true.
	I have known for many years
	That in her heart she does not love you.
KING:	Ye gods! Why have I deserved this?
	It is right that I lament.
	I thought I saw an angel
	When first I gazed upon her noble body;

	Is she really so cruel, that fell wife?	
	Truly, Cousin, I am confounded.	350
	Now go and bring her to me.	
	I must hear her speak.	
	[ROBBRECHT *goes to fetch the* QUEEN]	
ROBBRECHT:	Where are you, high-born lady?	
	Come to the king, my uncle.	
	[*Enter the* QUEEN, *crying*]	
	O noble lady, pull yourself together,	
	He is beside himself.	
	[*Enter* QUEEN *before the* KING]	
QUEEN:	O Lord King, noble lord,	
	Who will help us lament	
	The bitter sorrow that we bear,	
	Because we have lost our child?	360
KING:	Quiet and be damned,	
	Cruel whore, evil woman!	
	You have brought this pain and	
	These torments upon me!	
	It will not go easy for you,	
	For I know how it all happened,	
	How things got this way.	
	The foul deed was done by you alone,	
	You have murdered my beautiful child	
	And it will cost you your life,	370
	that you can be sure!	
	You are the most evil wife	
	Living on earth.	
QUEEN:	O noble Lord, noble King,	
	How should I be able	
	To cause pain	
	To the one I bore in my heart?	
KING:	Be still, evil woman, enough said,	
	I don't ever want to hear anything again.	

	I will drown you in a well	
	Robbrecht, take her to the prison!	380
	[*Exit* QUEEN *and* ROBBRECHT]	
QUEEN:	God, who let himself be crucified,	
	Help me now	
	And reveal my innocence,	
	For I know nothing about all this.	
ROBBRECHT:	Indeed, lady, it pains me.	
QUEEN:	O God, have pity on the great torment	
	I feel for I have lost my child	
	And they think I am to blame.	
	O, true God, on whom all things wait,	
	You were without friends and blameless,	390
	Nailed fast to a piece of wood	
	With three nails. Compassionate God,	
	Merciful God, now I pray,	
	Let the truth come out	
	And let my innocence be revealed.	
	This I pray to you also, Heavenly Queen.	
	O, it will be a miracle	
	If I don't go mad.	
	Who, O God, has turned his anger	
	So hatefully upon me?	400
	O God, from you flows	
	All justice and truth,	
	Now help me to the proof	
	That will reveal my innocence.	

[*Damascus, eighteen years later*]

ESMOREIT [*now a young man*]: O, Termagant and Apollo,
That noble lady, my sister,
Lives such a pure life,
Why is it that she loves no man,
Nor in all of the pagan land knows not one
She'd like for a husband?   410

By my God, Termagant,
She has a noble nature.
Perhaps she loves someone
Secretly, someone about whom I know nothing
Because she has never shown interest
In any man alive.
I wish Mohammed would give her a suitor
Equal to her noble nature.
    [*coming to an orchard*]
This is my dear sister's orchard,
Here's where she usually walks.   420
By my god Apollo,
I think I'll take my comfort here.
Ah . . . sleep overcomes me,
I'll lie here and take a rest.
    [*Enter* DAMIET *not seeing* ESMOREIT]

DAMIET: O me, O my, what great sorrow
I carry in my heart!
I am consumed by the love
I bear secretly.
O, Apollo, I lament to you.
In my heart I love a man   430
Who knows neither
His birth nor his parentage
And this makes my love even stronger.
Love has trapped me fast in her snare!
My father found him
And brought him to me as a young thing,
He gave him to me as a foundling
So that I could be his sister and his mother.
He thinks he is my brother,
But he is not so in the least.   440
I have loved him always and
Above all creatures,
He is noble in nature

And his spirit is lofty.
He is proud and, even though he was left
                                as a foundling,
I know in my heart
That he is descended from noble blood,
That he is high-born.
O Esmoreit, my dearest one,
Noble and courageous, beautiful hero,   450
Since my dear father found you—
It has been just
Eighteen years, I remember exactly—
You have been my beloved.
O dearest knight, O excellent one,
I will feel this sorrow forever
Because I cannot speak to you about it.
If I did, my father would take my life.

[Enter ESMOREIT *revealing himself to* DAMIET *having overheard her*]

ESMOREIT: O dearest and noble lady,
Am I a foundling?   460
I thought my lord the king,
Noble lady, was my father
And that you were truly my sister,
That we shared the very same blood.
But now ... O me, now I am forlorn!
By my God Termagant,
I am surely the unhappiest man
On earth.
O me, am I a foundling?
Surely there is no sadder man on earth.   470
I thought I was descended from a high lineage,
But now it seems I'm just a common wretch.
I pray you, noble ruby-lipped girl,
Tell me everything
From the beginning to the end,
Tell me how your father found me.

DAMIET:	O Esmoreit, truly excellent hero,	
	Now I am as unhappy as you.	
	I didn't know you were nearby	
	When I told this sad tale.	480
	O noble hero, do not take it wrongly,	
	I said it out of too much love.	
ESMOREIT:	O noble lady, now tell me	
	How things happened.	
	I want to say, "sister mine,"	
	But now I have to change all that	
	And learn another tune	
	By addressing you, "noble lady,"	
	As though I were a stranger.	
	Now and forever I must behave as your friend –	490
	You, trusted above all women	
	Who have been born on earth.	
	O noble lady, let me hear,	
	Tell me where I was found.	
DAMIET:	O, noble young man of high birth,	
	Now that you have heard the beginning	
	I will tell you the rest.	
	My father found you	
	In his orchard, excellent hero,	
	There where he used to walk.	500
ESMOREIT:	O, noble lady, tell me one thing,	
	Did you ever thereafter hear	
	A woman or a young lady lament	
	That she had lost her child?	
DAMIET:	O, noble and dearest youth,	
	This I have never heard.	
ESMOREIT:	Ah, then I must be of low birth	
	I think, or from a land far away.	
	Mohammed, help me clear	
	This blot, I must know	510
	Who did this to me,	
	How it happened that I was orphaned.	

	I will have no rest, night and day,	
	No peace, until I know	
	The family I come from	
	And who my father is.	
DAMIET:	O Esmoreit, please stay with me!	
	I beg you in the name of all women.	
	If my father should die, I will marry you,	
	Noble hero, you will be my husband.	520
	Then you, Esmoreit, will be	
	The great lord of Damascus.	
ESMOREIT:	O, noble lady, my disgrace	
	Will never touch you,	
	You must be spared the shame	
	Of marrying a foundling.	
	Your father is a great king,	
	And moreover, you are noble and beautiful,	
	More so than anyone alive,	
	You have the right to wear a crown.	530
	My heart trembles with shame	
	For what is happening to me.	
DAMIET:	O Esmoreit, leave off your grieving!	
	I pray you, noble hero.	
	Even if you were found by my father	
	It will never be held against you.	
	You and I, we will live	
	In great and immeasurable joy.	
ESMOREIT:	O noble lady, I am	
	Eternally grateful for this.	540
	I will never court	
	Another woman, not one who lives	
	In the world.	
	But first, by Termagant, I must	
	Find the father who conceived me	
	And the mother who bore me.	
	O ruby-lipped girl, I have said	
	Enough now, I must be gone.	

84   TEN NETHERLANDIC PLAYS

[ESMOREIT *retires to get his horse, armor, and provisions*]

DAMIET [*to herself*]: O me! I lament:
I am alone in my sorrow.   550
Too much talk does not help
That I know;
Too much talk usually
Makes for more sorrow,
And by saying too much, much has been lost.
Had I been quiet as a mouse,
I would have lived in bliss
With Esmoreit all my life,
But now, I have driven him away by
            speaking freely,
Rightfully I cry, alas!   560
O woe! that I have been so foolish
To speak these sad words.

ESMOREIT [*returning*]: O noble lady, now I will go.
Mohammed keep you pure.
Now I pray you, truly noble lady,
Say farewell for me to the King, my Lord,
For I will not return
Until I have found my family
And discovered the one who brought me here,
The one who made me an orphan.   570

DAMIET: O beautiful youth, Esmoreit,
Now I appeal to your compassion,
When you have discovered the truth,
Return again to me.

ESMOREIT: O beautiful young lady, free of heart,
Then I will never leave you again,
I will come to you,
Noble lady, the moment
I have discovered the truth,
By my God Termagant.   580

DAMIET: O Esmoreit, take this binding
In which you were swaddled

ESMOREIT 85

> When you were found.
> Noble youth, keep this for proof.
> Wrap it around your head,
> Display it openly,
> Perhaps someone
> Will recognize you by it.
> And remember me, truly excellent one,
> For I wait in great sorrow. 590

[ESMOREIT *leaves her*]

[*Some time later in Sicily, outside the prison*]

ESMOREIT: God, for whom nothing is hidden,
Be my comfort!
O, Mohammed and Apollo,
Mohammed and Termagant!
This beautiful blazon embroidered here,

[*looking at his swaddling clothes*]

I wish it belonged to me,
Then my heart would be free
Because I'd know I was born of noble blood.
Somehow I feel it is my coat of arms
Because I was wrapped in this cloth 600
When I was found as an orphan.
This must be my family's crest, the line of my birth —
My heart knows it's true
Because I was swaddled in this cloth.
But O, I will never have peace
Until I have found my ancestry
And the one who made me a foundling,
I'd like to thank him, by Apollo!
O, if only I could find my father and mother
My heart would overflow with joy. 610
And if they were of high birth,
Then I would be free of worry.

[*From her prison cell, the* QUEEN *overhearing him calls to* ESMOREIT]

QUEEN:	O noble youth, come to me now
	And speak to me a little while
	For I have heard you from far away,
	Sadly lamenting your sorrow.
ESMOREIT:	O beautiful lady, what has happened
	That you are kept in this prison?
QUEEN:	O noble youth, of noble heart,
	I must remain a prisoner forever 620
	Even though I've done no wrong,
	Accusation alone has done this.
	O beautiful child, now tell me,
	How did you come to this land
	And who gave you that turban?
	Tell me, truly excellent young man.
ESMOREIT:	By Mohammed my lord,
	I will not hide this from you, dear lady.
	We can tell each other our sorrows,
	For you are imprisoned 630
	And great sorrow has been dealt me,
	For I was made an orphan.
	And this turban is really
	The swaddling clothes in which I was wrapped,
	Dear lady, when I was found.
	I wear it for all to see
	On the chance that someone
	Who knew me may see it.
QUEEN:	Now tell me, truly excellent young man,
	Do you know where you were found? 640
ESMOREIT:	The truth is, dear lady, that I was discovered
	In an orchard in Damascus
	By the king — it was he who found me
	And later raised me.
QUEEN:	O God, who makes all things good,
	All praise unto you!
	My heart is overjoyed
	Because I have lived to see the day

	When I might see my child again.	
	My heart will break from joy,	650
	I see my child and hear him speak,	
	Him for whom I suffered such great torment.	
	Be welcome, truly dear child.	
	Esmoreit, I am your mother	
	And you are my child, this is certain	
	For I made that cloth	
	With my own hands, Esmoreit.	
	I wound you in it,	
	Esmoreit, just as when you were found,	
	Just as when you were taken from me.	660
ESMOREIT:	O, dear Mother, tell me without delay,	
	What is my father's name, he who begot me?	
QUEEN:	Sicily's greatest man	
	Is your father, excellent youth,	
	And the King of Hungary	
	Is my dear father.	
	You could not be of nobler birth,	
	In all of Christendom, near or far.	
ESMOREIT:	O, dear Mother, now tell me,	
	Why are you in prison?	670
QUEEN:	O dear child, that was done	
	By a slanderer, cruel and bitter,	
	Who made your father believe	
	That I had murdered you myself.	
ESMOREIT:	O me, the cruel villain	
	Who deceived my father the king,	
	Also delivered me up to despair	
	And made me an orphan.	
	O truly, if I knew who	
	It was that did this,	680
	He would die for it,	
	By my god, Apollo!	
	O dear mother mine,	
	I won't linger any longer,	

	I want to shorten your suffering:	
	I will go to my father, the high baron,	
	It will be my prayer	
	That he release you from this prison.	
	I give thanks to Mohammed and Apollo,	
	And the creator who made me	690
	And the mother who bore me	
	That I have found my family.	
	My heart rightfully rejoices	
	When I behold my mother.	
QUEEN:	Merciful God	
	Be praised and thanked in every way—	
	I have found my dear child,	
	He who will deliver me—	
	My heart overflows with	
	Immeasurable joy.	700

[*Sometime later in the palace in Sicily*]

ROBBRECHT [*aside*]: O me! a murdering thief
                                      caught in the act

	Is not as hopeless	
	As I am now,	
	I am in a shameful mess.	
	Had I killed him with my own two hands	
	When instead I sold him, he'd be dead.	
	I am terrified that	
	I will be made to suffer	
	Because if it comes out that I sold him	
	To a Saracen, I am lost.	710

[*Enter* KING]

KING:	Go hence, Robbrecht, my cousin,
	To my wife, the Queen,
	She, whom my heart must forever love.
	It is I who now must become her servant
	Because I have kept her prisoner
	Without deserving and without fault.

	My heart grieves many times over	
	Because I have been so cruel to her.	
	Go hence and bring her to me straight away,	
	And let her see her beautiful child.	720
ROBBRECHT:	Lord King, in true loyalty,	
	I will happily do so.	

[ROBBRECHT *at the prison*]

Come out of this prison, noble lady,
Where for so long you have been kept.
You will see the young prince,
Esmoreit, your young man.
My heart inwardly rejoiced
When I saw that excellent knight.

[*Back in the palace*]

KING:	O noble lady, give me your hand,	
	And please forgive me my misdeed,	730
	For the rest of my life	
	I will gladly be your servant,	
	For the fault is mine,	
	I understand that now,	
	For Esmoreit, our child, has come home,	
	A beautiful, grown-up youth.	
	I pray to God, who died	
	For love, to forgive me.	
QUEEN:	O noble lord, be of a free heart,	
	I am glad to forgive you	740
	For all my sorrow, all my torment,	
	And all my pain has been left behind.	
	Where is my dear child, Esmoreit?	
	Call him forth and let me see him.	
ROBBRECHT:	O noble lady, you shall see him.	
	Where are you Esmoreit, my cousin?	
ESMOREIT	[*entering*]: I am here, by Apollo!	
	O Mohammed, Mohammed,	
	Dear father, high baron,	

	I give you good day	750
	And also my mother, whom I never saw	
	Until a few moments ago.	
	I have lost all the sorrow	
	That burdened my heart.	
	When I learned I was a foundling,	
	I was the saddest of men	
	Alive on this earth,	
	But it has all worked out for the best!	
KING:	O Esmoreit, let me understand—	
	Tell me, where have you been living?	760
ESMOREIT:	With a king who wears the crown	
	Of Damascus, noble father.	
	He is a valiant Saracen	
	Who found me in an orchard,	
	And he has a high-born daughter	
	Who took care of me.	
	When her father, the king,	
	Found me, she became my mother	
	And treated me as her brother,	
	And it is she I love forever.	770
	She has told me everything,	
	How her father found me,	
	And that when her father brought me to her,	
	I lay swaddled in these bindings.	
QUEEN:	This is the cloth that I myself made,	
	Esmoreit, truly excellent youth.	
	I put your father's crest on it—	
	You can still see it in three quarters—	
	And also the crest of Hungary,[3]	
	Because that's part of your ancestry.	780
	I loved you so much, my son,	
	That I honored you with these designs,	
	But all turned to sorrow	
	When I lost you, Esmoreit.	
	I pray God, who chose the cross,	

	That He will forgive the one	
	Who gave me the bitter life	
	Which for so long I lived.	
ESMOREIT:	O, dear mother, by Apollo,	
	There was never a misdeed or a murder	790
	That did not come to light,	
	The deed will not go unpunished.	
ROBBRECHT:	By the Lord, who was crowned	
	With thorns,	
	Esmoreit, my cousin,	
	If I knew who had done this	
	He would die for it.	
	If he isn't already rotting in the grave,	
	I would kill him with my sword	
	And take his life.	800
	By god, if I knew the knave	
	Who did this shameful thing to you,	
	In all of Christendom	
	He'd find no safety.	
	Surely, he would die.	
QUEEN:	Now we will live in great joy	
	And forget all our sorrow	
	For my heart overflows	
	With joy unsurpassed.	
KING:	Esmoreit, son, now let us go	810
	And let us be happy,	
	But Mohammed and Apollo	
	You must abjure	
	And instead believe in Mary	
	And in God, the almighty father,	
	Who has made us all,	
	For everything on earth that lives	
	He has made through his art;	
	The sun and the moon, the day and night,	
	The heavens and the earth,	820
	Leaves and the grass alike,	

	All these he has made with his power;	
	In him you must believe.	
ESMOREIT:	Father, Lord, then I will pray to him,	
	The almighty God enthroned,	
	That he preserve	
	Damiet the beautiful	
	Above all who live,	
	For she has raised me,	
	And therefore it is right that I love her,	830
	The young Queen of Damascus,	
	Damiet, that noble lady.	
	O God, preserve her pure body,	
	For she is excellent and good.	
	It is right that I love her	
	Above all that live on this earth,	
	And if I didn't, I would be wretched	
	For she is my heart's companion.	
ROBBRECHT:	Esmoreit, cousin, she has earned your love.	
	Now let us forget all sorrow.	840
	In a happy humor let us dine,	
	For the table is ready.	

[*Meanwhile in Damascus*]

DAMIET:	O, where can Esmoreit be delayed	
	That he does not return?	
	I think that something terrible	
	has happened to him	
	Or that he has died a cruel death,	
	Or perhaps that he lives in great joy	
	And therefore has forgotten me.	
	In any event, I must know the truth,	
	What has happened to him,	850
	Even if it means that I have to travel	
	the world over to find him.	
	Where are you, Platus, wise counselor?	
PLATUS	[*entering*]: Noble lady, trusted and good,	

ESMOREIT 93

DAMIET:	I am at your service.	
	Meester Platus, I want to go	
	And look for Esmoreit country by country.	
	Even if it causes me injury,	
	Hunger, thirst or adversity.	
	It is something I must do,	
	True love presses me on.	860
	Dear Meester, I pray you	
	Don't hesitate to go with me,	
	Stay with me and give me advice,	
	As to how we might find him.	
PLATUS:	Lady, now be happy!	
	Seeing how you would look at him,	
	The youth you prize so highly,	
	I will go with you and search for this great man.	
DAMIET:	Platus, Meester, let us go then	
	Together disguised as pilgrims.	870

[*Sometime later in Sicily near the palace*]

	Greetings . . . Hello? Is there anyone here	
	Who will give us something,	
	Two pilgrims who have been driven out	
	And robbed by bandits?	
ESMOREIT	[*hearing her but not seeing her*]:	
	Is it possible that I hear Damiet's	
	Voice. Did I hear her?	
	O dear virgin, Saint Maria,	
	How is it that this voice sounds just like her?	
	Is it Damiet, my dearly beloved,	
	The beautiful Queen of Damascus,	880
	Whom I love above all women	
	Born on this earth?	
	Now speak again and let me hear	
	For you sound exactly like her.	
DAMIET	[*revealing herself*]: If I were in the kingdom	
	of Damascus,	

	Esmoreit, truly excellent youth,	
	Then I would look more like her,	
	But now I stand before you as a pilgrim.	
ESMOREIT:	O, Damiet, my wife,	
	Is it you, O noble lady?	890
	My heart, my soul and my body	
	May truly live in joy,	
	For I never saw or had a dearer guest	
	Of all those born on earth.	
	O, noble lady, let me hear,	
	How did you come to this country?	
DAMIET:	O, Esmoreit, truly excellent knight,	
	I wanted so much to see you	
	But I did not know where you were	
	And this caused me to suffer.	900
	So I disguised myself as a pilgrim,	
	And went as a wanderer through the country,	
	Taking Platus by the hand	
	That he could be my guard and guide.	
ESMOREIT:	Where are you, my dear father?	
	Come here, you must see her,	
	Who full of love and loyalty	
	Has born her heart to me.	
	It is right that I love her because	
	She has done so much for me.	910

[*Enter the* KING]

KING:	Therefore I will receive her with a happy heart.
	You are welcome, truly beautiful Damiet,
	You will wear a crown in Sicily
	Greater than all who live here
	For you will surely become my son's wife.
	This is the crown I have willed to my son
	For I am so old and
	Cannot wear it anymore.

[*Enter* ROBBRECHT]

ROBBRECHT:	Lord king, uncle, by Saint John,	
	Esmoreit is truly worthy of your gift.	920
	He is a knight whose fame is everywhere.	
	He handles weapons well.	
	It is good that he	
	Receive the crown from you.	
	Damiet, follow behind him,	
	And you will be the young Queen.	

[ROBBRECHT, DAMIET and the KING *withdraw upstage*]

PLATUS	[*aside to Esmoreit*]: Help, Mohammed!	
	Am I going crazy?	
	This is incredible!	
	O, Esmoreit, noble and free knight,	
	This is the man who brought you	930
	all your sorrow.	
	What he is telling you he does not mean,	
	He holds only ill will toward you.	
	I bought you from him for a thousand pounds	
	Of fine gold.	
ESMOREIT:	Meester, what are you telling me,	
	How did this happen?	
PLATUS:	O, Esmoreit, by Apollo,	
	It has been eighteen years	
	Since I came riding to this place	
	On this same horse, Esmoreit.	940
	Now hear what this villain did:	
	Surely, he would have strangled you,	
	He spoke such cruel words to you,	
	He said you were going to cost him the kingdom	
	And that you could not live for his sake.	
	All this I understood from his angry cries.	
ESMOREIT:	Meester, tell me the whole story,	
	Quickly, I pray you,	
	For I am already beside myself	
	Not knowing the truth—	950

	Who made my mother suffer so	
	And made me to languish in shame?	
PLATUS:	O Esmoreit, by Mohammed,	
	This same man has done it.	
	By my god Termagant,	
	He would have taken your life,	
	For he said so frankly, the caitiff,	
	I heard him and spoke to him	
	And told him that it would be an evil thing	
	To kill the young heir,	960
	That's when I bought you from him	
	For a thousand pounds of red gold.	
ESMOREIT:	By the Lord who made me,	
	Before I eat or drink	
	This misdeed will be revenged.	
	He will die now!	
	Where are you father, high baron,	
	And Robbrecht, the murderer?	

[*Enter* KING, QUEEN, DAMIET *and* ROBBRECHT]

ROBBRECHT:	By my lord, that is not true!	
	Esmoreit, my cousin,	970
	I have ever been good and true;	
	I was never a murderer or a traitor.	
ESMOREIT:	Quiet, you whore's son, for what you have done	
	Is even more evil!	
	How did it come into your mind	
	To sell your own flesh and blood	
	And to tell my father	
	That my mother had done it?	
ROBBRECHT:	I will fight a duel in my defense,	
	Esmoreit, truly noble hero,	980
	Is there anyone in this land	
	Who will challenge me to it?	
PLATUS:	Be still, evil tyrant,	
	You would have butchered him	

               Had I not heard you
               When I came riding up unannounced.
               I was never more glad
               As when I was able to buy the child from you.
               I gave you the uncounted money
               In a small box made of ivory.   990
               We still might find it hidden in your safe,
               I bet my life on it.
ESMOREIT: O me, Robbrecht, cruel villain,
               I have every right to hate you!
               Your doomsday has come,
               All the world cannot help you.

               Here they hang Robbrecht[4]

EPILOGUE

               [*Esmoreit turns to the audience*]
               And so it often happens,
               That cruel deeds are met with cruel ends,
               But pure hearts will wear the crown,   1000
               Those who know virtue and truth.
               Therefore I advise you, ladies and gentlemen,
               Set your lives on virtue,
               For you will ultimately be judged by God,
               There above in his high throne,
               Where the angels sing beautiful songs.
               He is our heavenly father!
               Now let us say, "Amen," together.
               Amen.
PLATUS: God, take us all in your protection.   1010
               Now hear, you wise and understanding people:
               Here you may observe and understand,
               How Esmoreit took his vengeance
               On Robbrecht, his cousin, here on this stage.
               Stay quietly seated everyone,
               No one should go home yet,

> Now we will play a farce for you
> Which will be short, I tell you.
> Who ever's hungry can go and eat.
> Go on down by these stairs.　　　　　　　　　　1020
> If you like it, then come again tomorrow.

Notes

1. Bastard in the sense of his being disinherited.
2. Balderijs, it has been suggested, may be a version of Bal(dac) Dar as(salem), the Arabic nickname for Bagdad. These kind of abbreviations were not uncommon in the Middle Ages. Roemans and van Assche (1967), 175–6; Romans and Gaspar (1954), 13.
3. The embroidery seems to be divided into quarters, three for Sicily, one for Hungary; or only three-quarters of the work can be seen after so many years of wear.
4. Original rubric.

Dissimulation: "carrying both fire and water," by P. Bruegel, from *Netherlandish Proverbs* or *The Blue Cloak*. Berlin-Dahlem, Staatliche Museen.

Lippijn

Dramatis Personae

Lippijn
His Wife
Her Lover
The Girlfriend (also known as "Trise")

Here begins the farce

[*In front of their house*]

WIFE: Hey, I say, hey! Thanks be to God!
[*aside*] I want to go and fool around
With my sweetie in the grass.
It's been days since I was with him.
Hey, I say, hey! Where are you Lippijn?
LIPPIJN [*entering*]: Here I am, what is it?
WIFE: Lippijn, you have to get water and fire,
And I'll go
And get us something to eat.
LIPPIJN: No you won't, by the death of our Lord, 10
you'll forget,
You always stay away so long.
WIFE: It's because I always have so much to do.
By the time the sermon ends
It's already late in the day.
And before I can go to the meat market
I have to wait 'til everyone
Has done their business —
So I can buy cheaply.
That's why I'm gone so long,
Lippijn, don't you get it? 20
LIPPIJN: Yeah, sure, you could tell me any story you like

	And I wouldn't know what to make of it.
	Go on, I'll lay the fire
	And get the water and scrub the pots,
	God help me, 'cause I'm stuck
	In a life of slavery.
WIFE:	Good Lippijn, and while you're at it,
	wash the dishes
	And make sure the floor is clean.
LIPPIJN:	Look, Honey, God keep you!
	And now hurry up. All my days I've 30
	Been your poor slave . . .
	And I think my future's not looking any better.
WIFE:	Shut up! God damn you.
	It kills me that you've lived this long!

[*Exit* LIPPIJN, WIFE *remains and moves down stage*]

[*to the audience*] I pulled that one off, didn't I?

[*She waits for some time*]

Where could my sweetheart be?
Hang him
For keeping me standing here waiting!

[*Enter, her lover*]

LOVER:	Sweetie pie, the craziest thing
	has happened to me.
	Have you been waiting here long? 40
WIFE:	Yeah, my heart's aching
	Waiting so long for you.
LOVER:	Let's go and get a tasty drink,
	My very best sweetheart.
	We'll be nice and comfy tonight,
	Come here, a little closer. . . .

[*Enter* LIPPIJN *observing them*]

LIPPIJN	[*to himself*]: O my Lord, I can't believe my eyes?
	By God, I've seen enough!
	There she is, lying there, with her knees bare,

LIPPIJN

               And he crawling between them.   50
               By the death of our Lord, he slid right in!
               Look at the whore, and she tried to
               Tell me she was hearing mass
               While she's lying here doing it
                            with another guy and
               Making me a horny John.
               She said she went to get meat.
               By Saint John, I'll make her pay for
               Her tricks tonight.
               I'll get a hold of a stick
               And beat her so hard   60
               She'll regret the little game
               She's playing with him!

[LIPPIJN *walks upstage and runs into his wife's* GIRLFRIEND]

GIRLFRIEND: Hey Lippijn! God give you good day!
             How are things? How are you?
LIPPIJN: O, Trise![1] I wish my heart would break
             Under the great sorrow I bear.
             Never again can I trust my wife
             After what she's done to me.
GIRLFRIEND: Lippijn, tell me, friend,
             What's happened?   70
LIPPIJN: I have been made a fool forever.
             She's off doing it with another man.
GIRLFRIEND: Come now, I can't believe that
             About your wife.
             I know how pure she keeps her body,
             She wouldn't do that for all the world.
LIPPIJN: What a man sees with his own two eyes
             Is hard for him to forget.
GIRLFRIEND: Lippijn, on my honor:
             Many are deceived by their eyes.   80
LIPPIJN: What? no, I'm not lying,
             I saw them myself

	Lying with bare knees,	
	Both of them going at it.	
GIRLFRIEND:	Lippijn, don't say that!	
	You will shame your wife.	
	Your eyes are worn out	
	With drinking and old age.	
	Good Lippijn, don't tell anyone this.	
	Your wife will be humiliated.	90
LIPPIJN:	What the devil. Would you make me blind	
	To things I saw myself?	
	I saw how she lay on her back	
	And how he lifted up her skirts.	
GIRLFRIEND:	Be quiet, good Lippijn,	
	It was not as you think.	
	Have you never heard of visions	
	That mislead and deceive us?	
	The fiend cares little for one lie	
	If he can make war between man and wife.	100
	I bet my life	
	That you saw a fairy.	
LIPPIJN:	Are you going to tell me that God has put	
	Elves and fairies in the world to plague us?	
	Is that it, you mean, it wasn't my wife?	
	That's really crazy!	
	I saw her with him.	
	He took her in his arms and pulled her to him.	
GIRLFRIEND:	Lippijn, a lie has never proven true.	
	I know your wife too well for this	110
	For she keeps her body pure.	
	She wouldn't do that for all the red and	
	sovereign gold in the world!	
	But fairy visions can be so powerful . . .	
	They blind many a man	
	So that he can't even recognize himself.	
	How could he then recognize anyone else?	

LIPPIJN:	By the death of our Lord,	
	you're driving me crazy!	
	What, has the devil possessed me?	
	Am I blind? Did I see nothing?	
	That's news to me!	120
	I see these people	
	Sitting around us here clear as day!	
	You see, I'm not completely blind,	
	Even though you'd like to make me think I am.	
GIRLFRIEND:	Lippijn, do you know what you're doing?	
	I pray you never again to say such things,	
	And to treat your wife with respect.	
	It is a fairy who's tormenting you,	
	Who's put you beside yourself and	
	Screwed your eyes up.	130
LIPPIJN:	Ah friend, is that what's bothering me?	
	But I was sure that I saw her.	
GIRLFRIEND:	It was a fairy who lay there,	
	That I will swear on the cross.	
	Your wife is back in her house,	
	I'll bet you a beer.	
LIPPIJN:	But she asked me to go get water and fire and	
	She said she went to get food.	
GIRLFRIEND:	Well Lippijn, if you want to know the truth,	
	They really pulled a fast one this time.	140
	A fairy spread a net	
	To catch you in, that I know for sure.	
	Come with me, let's go to your door.	
	Your wife will be sitting by her fire.	
LIPPIJN:	Is it beer that's made me see these things	
	Or do fairies really fly in the streets?	

                [*They walk to* LIPPIJN's *house*]

GIRLFRIEND:	Hey girl, can you let us in?
WIFE:	Yeah, sure, who's there?
GIRLFRIEND	[*aside*]: Well, Lippijn didn't I tell you the truth?

LIPPIJN:	Blessed God of heaven,	150
	I never saw a miracle like this.	
	I see now that I was wrong.	
GIRLFRIEND:	What did I tell you, Lippijn,	
	But you didn't want to believe me.	
	My friend is loyal and good,	
	Even if you'd like to make her out to be a whore.	
WIFE:	God give him a cramp in his jaw!	
	Is that what he said about me?	
GIRLFRIEND:	Yup, and that you were laying another guy,	
	That's what he told me.	160
LIPPIJN:	Really, Honey, I thought I saw it!	
	But now I'm satisfied.	
	Trise knows how to put it all together.	
	But on my life	
	I was sure you got up this morning	
	And asked me to get fire and water.	
WIFE:	Shut up, you stupid ass,	
	So, I'm doing it with another guy, eh?	
LIPPIJN:	Yeah, if you want to know the truth,	
	Either my eyes were screwed up or	170
	that's what I saw.	
	But Trise showed me	
	That an evil spirit deceived me.	
WIFE:	Why did you slander me then	
	And spread my shame all over the place?	
LIPPIJN:	O sweetie, I'll fix it	
	If I've done you any harm.	
WIFE:	Right! But you'll still get a beating for it,	
	You dirty, mean old goat.	
GIRLFRIEND:	By our Lord, he deserves to	
	Be trampled under our feet.	180
LIPPIJN:	Sweet wife, I'll never say it again.	
	I didn't know I was crazy.	
WIFE:	Yeah, I'll teach you to go around blabbering!	
	Here they fight[2]	

EPILOGUE[3]

> Dear friends, we have
> Played for you a farce.
> There are those — you know well —
> Who have seen something like this.
> You know that many funny things like this
> > are seen
> About which nothing more is said. 190
> Therefore I hope that you truly have found
> Meaning in our little jokes.
> I pray God, who is full of mercy,
> Who was born of a virgin,
> That no one will be put out
> By what he has seen or understood here.
> Get up, you can go out,
> For we must part.
> Our Lord God must guide us all.
> Amen. 200

NOTES

[1] The girlfriend's name is "Trise," a version of Theresa.
[2] Original rubric.
[3] It is not indicated who the speaker is here.

Flemish tapestry, "A Noble Company," documenting the influence of Islamic and Oriental elements in the fashions of the Middle Ages. The Cloisters, New York.

GLORIANT

An abel spel, an excellent thing,
About the Duke of Bruuyswijc,
And how he fell in love
With the daughter of the Red Lion of Abelant
And the farce which follows it.

Dramatis Personae

GLORIANT, the Duke of Bruuyswijc
GHERAERT, his uncle
GODEVAERT, a counselor,
RED LION, the King of Abelant
FLORENTIJN, daughter to the King of Abelant
ROGIER, messenger and servant to Florentijn
FLOERANT, nephew to the king of Abelant
A HANGMAN

PROLOGUE

> I ask God, the great Father,
> That He preserve us all.
> Ladies and gentlemen, great and small,
> I bid you all
> To be still,
> And mark this, you who are interested.
> We will play for you a noble thing,
> About a high-born youth,

Who was the Duke of Bruuyswijc.
He thought that no one 10
Living on this earth could be his match;
He spoke his thoughts proudly,
Boasting and imprudent words,
That often bring many a man to shame.
For he who puffs himself up too much,
If then things turn out differently,
Will be ashamed of his bragging.
And so it happened to this noble hero, who,
Even though he was rich and high-born,
Came to regret his boasting. 20
For because of his vanity,
Lady Venus became angry with him,
So that afterwards she wreaked havoc on him
For the proud words he spoke,
As you now will see.
Therefore I advise, ladies and gentlemen,
That no one brag about himself too much,
Because seldom will it be good.
Too much pride will never be praised.
Now I pray to God, who was slain 30
On the cross for our sins,
That we will find peace
In the sweet Valley of Josaphat,
Where God will sit in judgment.[1]
This I pray to Maria, the Queen.
Now listen and be quiet, we are starting.

                [*Bruuyswijc*]

GHERAERT: Where are you, dear friend Godevaert?
GODEVAERT: I am here, lord Gheraert.
Tell me, how can I serve you?
GHERAERT: Godevaert, I think it is time that 40
The duke, our noble baron,
Chose a wife

              And got himself married.
              He is noble and true,
              And he's the bravest young man of our time.
              If he had a wife she would bear
              Children for the good of our country,
              This vast and great land,
              For it would truly be a shame if he died
                                  without an heir.
              I 've called on you,   50
              To give me some advice in this matter.
GODEVAERT: Lord Gheraert, I have considered your idea,
              And it would indeed be good for us all,
              But I tell you plainly,
              Lord Gheraert, you are the Duke's uncle
              And therefore you can serve him
              Better than I who am not related to him.
GHERAERT: But now Godevaert, you must give us advice
              As to how we should proceed.
              The country would prosper indeed   60
              If he had a wife and children as well.
GODEVAERT: Yes, Lord Gheraert, therefore, let's you and me,
              Between the two of us, find a way. . . .
              I know someone
              We could certainly present to him.
              The King of Auvergne
              Has a daughter, excellent and good;
              She is pure and royal,
              And she is descended from a noble line.
GHERAERT: Indeed, Lord Godevaert,   70
              That marriage-match sounds good to me.
              The King of Auvergne comes from noble blood
              And in his day
              He always bore his arms proudly.
              His ancestors were great men.
              Indeed, Godevaert,
              This sounds like a match made in heaven.

GODEVAERT: Then let's go to the Duke
And tell him about it
So we can hear 80
What he thinks of it.
Now let us go, you and me,
To hear what he says.
If his heart welcomes it
Then we will arrange the marriage.
Where are you Duke, high-born man,
Noble Duke of Bruuyswijc?

[*Enter* GLORIANT]

GLORIANT: Make yourselves at home, uncle,
And my dear friend, Godevaert!
Now tell me dear uncle, Gheraert, 90
What do you desire, for truly you shall have it.

GHERAERT: Gloriant, my nephew, we would like to see
You get married.
We would welcome it with joy, noble baron,
As would your country, Bruuyswijc.

GLORIANT: Uncle Gheraert, high-born hero,
I am not ready for this.
I pray you not to bother me with it
Because I don't want to hear about it.
I know no woman on earth 100
With whom I'd like to spend my life.

GHERAERT: Nephew, you must consider the good
              of the country
As well as your own desires.
You will have to take a wife,
Nephew, in order to have children.

GODEVAERT: I can't keep my mouth shut any longer!
Noble Duke, high-born baron,
You must do it for your country,
To have children, everything Gheraert says.
It is a thing not usually done, 110

| | To remain a great lord without a wife.
| | You would dishonor your country,
| | Noble Lord, if you died without an heir;
| | There would be uprisings and discord,
| | Everyone would want to be the next ruler.
| | You would be the cause of great suffering
| | To this noble country, Bruuyswijc.
| GLORIANT: | Godevaert, Godevaert, really
| | Your reasoning's no good —
| | Not one woman has ever touched my heart;   120
| | There's not one I'd give two cents for.
| | Truly, I know no woman
| | That I would make my wife.
| GODEVAERT: | Lord, be careful that you do not come to regret
| | The foolish words you utter.
| | If Lady Venus gets angry at you,
| | She will make you her dupe.
| GHERAERT: | Gloriant, my nephew, listen carefully:
| | Samson the mighty hero
| | Was deceived by the workings of love;   130
| | And so was Absalom, the fair,
| | And the wise king, Solomon,
| | All were foold by love.
| | These are no lies but eternal truths,
| | The love of women conquered them.
| GLORIANT: | Really, uncle, it amazes me
| | That they were so foolish.
| | Uncle, Gheraert of Normandy,
| | There must have been other things involved,
| | For surely they were not the masters   140
| | of their own hearts
| | If they were made crazy for the love of women.
| | I myself know no woman of such high birth
| | That I'd give even two pence for her.
| GHERAERT: | Truly, nephew, anyone
| | Who'd listen to you would laugh;

	I have never heard such foolish words	
	Spoken by a high born man.	
	Never mind, nephew, you must	
	Marry for the good of your country.	
GLORIANT:	Truly, uncle, no man	150
	Will ever see the time	
	When I will take a wife,	
	No woman who now lives on this earth,	
	No woman who lives anywhere in this world.	
	For I have such a noble body	
	That if I should lie with a woman	
	I would thereafter always be out of sorts.	
	I am the great lord	
	Of this country, Bruuyswijc, and	
	There is no woman on earth who is my equal.	160
	I want to remain my own man.	
GHERAERT:	By the father who begot me,	
	This is really a foolish tale.	
	Really, nephew, it does not become you	
	To speak so lowly of women.	
GODEVAERT:	Yes, Gheraert, you are right.	
	He has spoken against women,	
	But love will revenge himself on him,	
	That I know for sure.	
	A sweet glance from the right woman	170
	Will surely be medicinal.	
GLORIANT:	Uncle Gheraert, by my troth,	
	This will never happen.	
	My heart is as hard as a stone and	
	Guards my noble body.	
	I know no woman on earth	
	Who I think is worthy of me.	
	My heart is like a falcon flying	
	Above the love of any woman.	
	Why would I give over my heart	180
	And my five senses to the power of a woman?	

| | God punish me
| | If ever I do that.
| GHERAERT: | Gloriant, nephew, all my urgings
| | Are for naught, I understand that.
| | But wait, you may still regret
| | This talk, this foolish tale.

[*Meanwhile, in Abelant*[2]]

| FLORENTIJN | [*alone*]: Truly indeed, there is no man born
| | On earth who is my equal,
| | Who is my like in nature,   190
| | Who shares my temperament.
| | I have never seen a man so rich in possessions
| | That I would take him as my husband,
| | Neither an emir nor a sultan,
| | Not any high-born enough.
| | No one who has proposed to me
| | Was good enough for me to accept his love.
| | Still . . . I heard the same thing is true
| | About a man in Christendom,
| | The Duke of Bruuyswijc.   200
| | I've heard that his heart is so courageous
| | And his nature so proud
| | That he, in the same way, does not love
| | a single woman.
| | We are of the selfsame mind,
| | (That my heart can tell right away).
| | We were born under the same planet,
| | And together share the same nature.
| | I will send him a portrait
| | A likeness made of my appearance.
| | If we two are alike,   210
| | Then his heart will get the better of him.
| | By my god, Termagant,
| | I'd like to hear what he might desire,
| | For, because his heart is so proud,

My heart is quite disposed to him.
> [*Calling*]

Where are you Rogier, my messenger?
Come to me, I have something for you to do.
> [*Enter* ROGIER]

ROGIER: O noble lady, by Mohammed,
Tell me, what is your wish?

FLORENTIJN: Rogier, you must go quickly 220
To the Duke of Bruuyswijc
Who lives in Christendom.
He is called Gloriant.
You will give the noble hero
This portrait of me, put it in his hands,
And tell him that I had it made
Exactly to my likeness,
And that you come from the kingdom,
Of the city of Abelant.
And tell him also, the noble hero, 230
I pray with all due respect
That he, in honor of all women,
Examine this figure carefully.
He will surely wonder
What I might mean by that.
And tell him that I've never seen a man
With whom I'd share my life,
And at the same time tell him
That my father is the high baron
Of Abelant, the Red Lion. 240
Then be cunning and still, listen and hear
everything,
And remember exactly what he tells you,
And then bring me his message.

ROGIER: By my God, Termagant,
Lady, this errand will be done,
I will make haste to go.

[*Exit* ROGIER]

[*Sometime later in Bruuyswijc,* ROGIER *meets* GLORIANT]

    Mohammed and Apollo,
    Protect my lady
    Who has sent me here.
    Noble lord, I am a messenger 250
    From a young lady who is excellent and good.
    She prays you with due respect
    To look upon this figure.
    It is made after the most beautiful creature
    One can find on earth,
    And her likeness is exactly the same
    As if she were really the woman herself,
    She is famous for her virtue
    And also for her great spirit.

GLORIANT: Messenger, now tell me 260
    Who is this young lady? Tell me more.

ROGIER: This is Florentijn of Abelant,
    A noble and rich young lady.
    Her equal cannot be found in any pagan land.
    She is so excellent and her body so fair
    That on earth there are not five women who are
    The equal of my lady.
    She could not be more excellent,
    Cultivated, nor better formed.
    Her body is so perfect 270
    And her character so upright that
    There is no one born on earth
    Who is rich and high-born enough for her;
                                   no one
    Who has been able to gain her love,
    To make her his wife.
    She is a virgin, chaste and pure,
    And she has a father of great fame,
    Who is, you know,

	The Red Lion of Abelant.	
GLORIANT:	You are a good and loyal messenger	280
	That I can see.	
	Now come and go with me,	
	That I may show you my hospitality.	
ROGIER:	Gladly will I go, noble baron.	

[*They go to the palace;* GLORIANT *remains outside alone*]

GLORIANT:	Now I pray God, who has the power,	
	That He let me live to see the day	
	When I may meet this young lady face to face.	
	She has honored me with her friendship	
	And sent me this portrait	
	With her likeness printed upon it.[3]	290
	O God may her face	
	Be like this portrait, for	
	In the whole world I have never seen her equal.	
	In Bruuyswijc she would be worthy	
	To be a lady and a duchess.	
	God, in whom all goodness lies,	
	Bless her every day.	
	O God, what powers lie hidden in her heart,	
	Things even more excellent than I know!	
	Her nobility is her crowning glory,	300
	More excellent than any other woman.	
	O God bless her,	
	She who sent me this treasure.	
ROGIER	[*entering*]: O high-born hero,	
	I have brought my message to you,	
	Now I want to return	
	To my lady, Florentijn.	
GLORIANT:	Rogier, Rogier, now be	
	Good and trustworthy in every way,	
	Speak highly	310
	About what you've heard and seen here.	
	But be sure not to tell the others,	

Rogier, about the task I will give you.
One who can keep secret, he is a messenger
                              to be praised.
Dear Rogier, be trustworthy,
And give my best to your beautiful young lady
And tell her truthfully
That no woman has had from me
A proposal of love but she alone for
She is so pure   320
And her nature is so noble.
Then tell the excellent and beautiful lady
That she preserve her chastity for me,
For the happiness of us both,
And I will be true to her.

ROGIER: O noble lord, by Apollo,
She bid me to ask you
Explicitly, noble lord,
If she would ever see you.

GLORIANT: She shall, Rogier.   330
Before seven weeks have passed,
I will see the young lady and speak to her,
If God protects my life.
Give my warmest greeting to that noble lady,
Who God must always preserve.

ROGIER: Now I will go quickly.
Mohammed and Apollo,
Mohammed and Jupiter,
Bless me and keep me.

             [*Sometime later in Abelant*]

FLORENTIJN: Rogier, now bring me the news,   340
Have you seen this high-born man?

ROGIER: Yes, lady, by Termagant,
He is a man of great worth.
I am certain that his equal
Does not live on earth

Nor does the world possess
One more fair or more noble.
He is a man of princely blood,
Rich in possessions, great in ancestry.
He is nobly born and his power is mighty. 350
He keeps a rich court.
I have never heard so much praise
Given as they give Gloriant.
He is truly a courageous hero
And for all men formidable.

FLORENTIJN: Rogier, Rogier, tell me then,
What greetings has he sent me?
ROGIER: O noble and celebrated lady,
He told me truthfully
That no woman ever received from him 360
A proposal of love except you alone,
And he bids you, noble pure lady,
That you preserve your chastity for him
To the happiness of you both. In return,
                                  he promises
To be true to you.
FLORENTIJN: Tell me Rogier, by Apollo,
Did he not say that he would like to see me?
ROGIER: Yes, lady, you will have what you want.
Before seven weeks have passed
You will see him and speak to him. 370
That's what the noble hero told me.
He pledged it to me with a handshake
And swore to me that he would be true.
FLORENTIJN: By my god, Apollo,
I will wait for that time to come.
It will be just as I expected,
And I will see it indeed;
When I will look at the duke,
Then I will be free of all sorrows.
Rogier, get up and go with me 380

You have delivered your message well.
[Meanwhile, in Bruuyswijc]

GLORIANT: Where are you, noble uncle, Gheraert
Of Normandy high-born?
I need your advice,
Noble uncle, high-born hero.
GHERAERT: What did you say, nephew Gloriant,
What is it you are wanting?
GLORIANT: Noble uncle, I can no longer hide it,
My heart is pierced.
True love is making me suffer so much 390
That it will cost me my life.
I love a noble woman so deeply
That for hours, day and night,
I cannot rest. I cannot sleep
Since first my love for her began.
GHERAERT: Now here's something I can't believe!
What ever could have happened
To make your noble heart suffer
Sorrow over a woman?
One who lives on this earth? 400
I cannot believe it!
GLORIANT: O noble uncle of great fame,
Truly I do suffer and it's my fault
Because in the past I often repeated
Those stupid words.
Noble uncle, now it is revenged
That I spoke foolishly.
The lady Venus is angry at me
And she has hit me in my heart
And made me a lover of women 410
And taught me to follow the path of love.
GHERAERT: How can I believe this?
You bore such a proud demeanor,
You told Godevaert and me

That no woman on earth
Is born so high or so rich
That you'd think her worthy of you.
Your "heart flies just like a falcon
Above the power of love."
Love couldn't have entered into you mind! 420
You're making me laugh!
I know that your heart is so full of pride
That no woman could catch you!

GLORIANT: O noble uncle, understand me,
I spoke so foolishly
Because I lacked all
Knowledge of the real truth.
Now I come for mercy to all women
Because there is one who pains me;
My heart and desire, my soul and spirit, 430
Are all in the power of one young lady.

GHERAERT: Who is the young lady that makes you suffer so?
Gloriant, nephew, tell me,
Because I still can't forget
The proud words you spoke.
Did you fall in love despite them?
Really, nephew, this amazes me!
Tell me now who is she,
The one who has wounded your heart?

GLORIANT: Uncle, Gheraert of Normandy, 440
Noble uncle, courageous hero,
Her name is Florentijn of Abelant,
She has a father of great fame.
The Red Lion of Abelant,
You know, is her father.

GHERAERT: Help, Lord God of paradise!
Nephew, how can that be?
It's incredible
Because she lives so far from here.

GLORIANT: O, noble uncle, the fire of love 450

Travels much faster than a bow shot.
Uncle Gheraert, by my God,
She sent me a message
With a portrait, her likeness,
A figure exactly like her own.
She is the most beautiful creature
Living under the vault of heaven.
She is worthy to wear the crown
Even of the King of France,
No woman on whom the sun 460
Now shines is her equal.
Even though my heart suffers because of her,
Truly, uncle, she is worth it.
She is renowned for her virtue
And also for her lofty spirit.
O noble uncle, now you know
The state of my deepest secret.
Now I pray you, uncle, advise me
On how to win my beloved.

GHERAERT: Gloriant, nephew, that day 470
You will never see
For you must love another.
I will tell you the reason why.
The Red Lion is distinguished
And a man of great might,
But he hates our ancestors
Above all who live on earth,
Because with my own sword
I slew his father there in Abelant.
And your father, that mighty hero, 480
Killed his uncle, Eysenbaert,
The most courageous man ever born
To take up his sword in pagan lands.
But your father, widely revered,
Slew him, cutting his neck in two.
And your father caused him even more pain—

                And about this he never laughed —
                Your father slew two of his beautiful children,
                The ones who were born in Antioch.
                This grieves the Red Lion still,   490
                That I know truly.
                Even if you were lord of all of Christendom
                The Red Lion would not give you his daughter.
GLORIANT: By God who let himself be crucified,
                Uncle, Gheraert of Normandy,
                And by Mary, saint and virgin,
                I shall have her or die,
                Even if he is my greatest enemy
                Greater still than I.
                He who is not strong must be clever.   500
                I will win that pure lady.
                With my own body,
                I intend to claim her, God permitting.
GHERAERT: Gloriant, my nephew, all jesting aside,
                How do you plan to do that?
GLORIANT: That I will tell you, noble man,
                Courageous hero of Normandy,
                I will ride disguised
                As a knight errant.
                I will overcome the trials of love   510
                And do everything to get the beautiful Florentijn.
                In the meantime, noble uncle, stay loyal
                To the good country of Bruuyswijc
                For no one alive is your equal,
                Dear uncle.
                I pray that you do not waiver,
                Be true to this good country
                And stand fast though my shame may spread,
                This I pray you noble uncle, Gheraert.
                If I should die on the journey   520
                Then the country is yours.
                Now, God be with you, courageous hero,

	I must begin my journey.	
GHERAERT:	O Gloriant, my nephew,
	I think you will regret this voyage.
	You can find many more beautiful women
	In Christendom, high baron.
	The Red Lion is cruel.
	I know it well, child. If he finds out who you are
	He will remember that your father destroyed	530
	His kin in Abelant and then
	He will make you suffer,
	Truly nephew, I know this well.
GLORIANT:	Come what may, uncle,
	This journey must be undertaken.
GHERAERT:	So may you succeed,
	This I pray to God in heaven.
	Gloriant, nephew, God reward you!
	Now be clever and plan carefully.
	Keep your disguise up	540
	And let no one know who you are,
	Say little,
	And make your words resolute and deliberate;
	Do not act rashly
	Or you will come into misery.
	And when you come upon what you have
	your heart set on,
	The good lady, Florentijn,
	Show yourself as a nobleman.
	And remember always,
	I am a father to you	550
	As long as God will keep me alive.
	Still, if you'd quit this journey
	You'd be acting wisely. . . .
GLORIANT:	No, Uncle, not for all that is good,
	Not for all that the sun's rays touch . . .
	I will not forget her, I will see
	Florentijn, the noble lady.

	Where is my horse, Valentine?	
	I want to go right away.	
	Noble uncle, trusted and good,	560
	I put my lands in your power,	
	That you will keep them loyally	
	Until I return from Abelant.	
GHERAERT:	O, noble nephew, Gloriant,	
	God our Lord protect you	
	And always keep you virtuous	
	Wherever you go.	

[*Exit* GHERAERT; GLORIANT *journeys to Abelant*]

GLORIANT [*alone*]: O God, I now see
How painful it is to learn to serve love.[4]
Before I loved that beauty, Florentijn,   570
My heart stood as an enemy against all women.
But now in my heart
All women are exalted; only Florentijn,
That pure lady, could have done this,
She who taught me the way of love.
O almighty God, I thank you for love,
You who came down from heaven
And took upon yourself a human shape,
You who from a maid, a sovereign woman,
Received a human body   580
Which you let hang on the wood
Without having deserved it. Guiltless,
You let your noble heart be broken
With a lance pierced through.
You did all this by the power of love.
O God, what wonder you caused,
All of it emanating from true love!
That's why those who know love's ways
Don't discourage me
Even though love causes me so much pain.   590
For love is so powerful,

That she made the strong and almighty God
Descend from heaven
To pay our debt for us.
This was all done by love's craft.
And so he chose Mary, that noble vessel,
The enclosed garden,
Wherein was hidden the treasure
That ransomed us
And brought us out of eternal damnation.   600
O love, you are the noblest flower,
You bear the sweetest fruit
That God makes grow upon the earth.

> [*Arriving in Abelant*]

Now I am in Abelant, the beautiful city
Where my lady lives,
But the place seems to be locked up,
Which makes sense since it's two o'clock at night;
I suspect that there's a guard on watch. They say,
"Where the watch is good, there is peace."
Abelant, Abelant, dearest of cities.   610
Because I may not enter you yet,
I'll wait till tomorrow morning
And take my nightly rest here.
Valentine can graze on the grass
Until the sun comes up.

> [GLORIANT *lies down in an orchard and sleeps,*
> *while* FLORENTIJN *looks out of her window above and sees him*]

FLORENTIJN: Thanks be to Mohammed and Apollo!
I see a high-born falcon
Has descended into my orchard,
The one I have waited for so long.
He is wearing a sign   620
By which I recognize him.[5]
O, when I look at him I know
He is the one I truly love.

Let me go and welcome him warmly
For he, the noble falcon from Christendom,
The high baron of Bruuyswijc,
Has descended on my hand.
[*going down*] I saw the courageous hero
                                  go this way
To his horse in the pasture.
    [*Enter* FLORENTIJN *into the orchard*]
Welcome you are, Gloriant,   630
For you have captured my heart!
I saw you by the light of the moon,
I overheard your language,
And I recognized you immediately
By the sign you wear.

GLORIANT: O Florentijn, truly beautiful maid,
You have spoken well, noble and pure lady;
I prayed to the God of Nazareth
To preserve your chastity.
O Florentijn, truly excellent lady,   640
I suffered much for your sake!
What adventures have I had
Before arriving in your country!

FLORENTIJN: O, noble duke Gloriant,
You are most welcome here!
Your fame is justified, for
On all the earth I never saw a man
Who made my heart more joyful
Than you, high baron.
But if my father, the Red Lion, knew   650
That we two were in this orchard together,
By my god Apollo
We would both loose our lives![6]

GLORIANT: God, who was born of the Virgin,
Must be protector of us both!
O chosen one, Florentijn,

                Ideal higher than all women,
                Will all I have suffered for you
                Have been in vain?
                I have left my country   660
                Just to talk to you, pure lady,
                And I come to you wandering alone
                Like a poor page.
FLORENTIJN: O Gloriant, it is unjust,
                By my god Termagant!
                But it is right that he who genuinely
                And truly loves
                Will win his love in return.
                In the same way that I have received
                                      love from you,
                Now you will also receive from me   670
                All that your noble heart desires,
                In all purity, worthy knight,
                Entirely without shame.
GLORIANT: By the Virgin Saint Mary,
                Truly sovereign Florentijn,
                For all the riches of the earth
                I would not disgrace you.
                But, noble lady, prepare yourself
                To journey with me to Bruuyswijc,
                For we cannot dally here much longer.   680
                If your father, the Red Lion, knew it,
                He would make us both suffer
                So that we'd be unhappy forever.
FLORENTIJN: O noble duke Gloriant
                I would gladly see Bruuyswijc
                If I could do so honorably,
                Then I would go where you desire.[7]
GLORIANT: O Florentijn, worthy lady,
                Whom I love above all women,
                I will make you Duchess of   690
                The good country, Bruuyswijc,

	Take my honor as your proof,	
	Noble high-born lady.	
FLORENTIJN:	Then I will go on this voyage with you,	
	Man above all men who live,	
	Or any I have seen with my own eyes,	
	Noble duke, high baron.	
	Now let us wait here in this orchard	
	Until the moon is gone,	
	And they will all be asleep,	700
	Everyone who belongs to my father's court,	
	Then we can go without trouble,	
	Without seeing anyone.	
GLORIANT:	O, noble lady, that is a good plan,	
	For I am so overcome with sleep	
	That I can no longer stand.	
	In any case, I must rest my head.	
FLORENTIJN:	Then lay your head down in my lap	
	And sleep, high-born hero,	
	And then we will leave Abelant.	710

[*Enter* FLOERANT *unobserved by the lovers*]

FLOERANT:	What! Mohammed and Apollo!	
	Can it be that the young lady, Florentijn,	
	Has grown so foolish?	
	Of all the princes in pagan lands	
	She could love not one,	
	No matter how high-born or how rich;	
	She would not give her heart to any one!	
	But now she loves a Christian	
	And wants to run away with him!	
	Unless I keep quiet about this,	720
	She will be dishonored forever. . . .	
	By my god, Termagant,	
	No! . . . I will tell her father	
	What I have seen and heard!	

[*Exit* FLOERANT *in search of the* RED LION]

	Where are you, high-born baron	
	Of Abelant, Lord Red Lion?	
	Get up, high-born man,	
	And quickly put on your clothes,	
	For I will tell you something you don't know.	
RED LION	[*entering*]: Here I am, on the spot,	730
	Floerant, nephew, what is the matter?	
FLOERANT:	O noble uncle, I have seen	
	A strange thing. The beautiful Florentijn,	
	Who is worthy to wear the crown	
	Of the sultan of Babylon,	
	Is lying in the orchard,	
	In the arms, courageous hero,	
	Of a man from Christendom,	
	The famous Duke of Bruuyswijc.	
	I will show you	740
	Where he lies next to the noble lady,	
	World renown, noble hero,	
	For I have stolen his sword	
	And I have secretly taken away	
	His horse, who's called Valentine.	
	He has come that way from Bruuyswijc[8]	
	Where he is the Duke.	

[*They come to the orchard*]

	Now see, high-born man,	
	How he lies in her lap.	
RED LION:	I can't believe it!	750
	My daughter Florentijn!	
	Was there no Saracen noble enough	
	To capture her heart?	
	Instead she lies here with a Christian	
	Who does not know our laws![9]	
	O, why has she done this to herself,	
	Lowered herself so shamelessly!	
	By my god Termagant,	

	She will burn for this in the fire,	
	And the Duke will not escape either!	760
	I will capture him	
	And hang him from a tree,	
	By my god Apollo!	
	Let's go, Floerant, my nephew,	
	And let us surprise the noble Baron.	
FLOERANT:	O noble uncle, that won't be difficult,	
	For he is without his weapon.	
	[*standing over* GLORIANT] Get up,	
	high-born nobleman	
	Noble hero of Bruuyswijc!	
	In Abelant, this sweet state, this beautiful jewel,	770
	There is a hidden castle	
	Where you will live	
	And be the keeper.	
	It stands on a such a beautiful square	
	The likes of which no man has seen.[10]	
GLORIANT	[*starting up*]: By God you will be punished,	
	Cruel Saracen, foul caitiff!	
	By my faith, you have over-stepped your bounds	
	And it will cost you your life.	
FLOERANT:	O noble lord of great distinction	780
	Forget your heroic plans,	
	Too much pride is never good.	
	You will be caught	
	And then we will take your life	
	For you have earned your death.	
GLORIANT	[*looking at him*]: Alas, I did not foresee	
	this trickery,	
	I have lost my sword!	
	God, who was born of Mary,	
	Punish the one who took it,	
	The one who came to me secretly	790
	While I lay in such happiness.	
	I am right to mourn	

	The loss of my sword,	
	For by my honor, if I had it in my hands	
	You would not catch me, foul caitiff!	
RED LION:	Lord duke, forget these words and stay,	
	Your anger is useless.	
	You will have to pay	
	For what your ancestors have done.	
	Before Abelant I saw my father	800
	Beaten by your kinsman,	
	Gheraert of Normandy, it was he,	
	Who slew my dear father;	
	And your father, by Apollo,	
	Slew my uncle, Eysenbaert.	
	And then there were two knights of high birth	
	Whom your mighty father slew,	
	(My beautiful children, if you must know,	
	Who where born in Antioch)	
	You will have to pay for this,	810
	By my god, Apollo!	
	And my daughter, Florentijn,	
	I shall kill by fire.	
GLORIANT:	O noble lord of Abelant,	
	Do with me what you wish.	
	But spare Florentijn, who is worthy	
	To wear the crown of any noble man,	
	For by the father who begot me,	
	She is a still maid.	
	In the hours that have passed	820
	She has not yet been any man's wife.	
	She is a noble creature.	
	Be merciful to her, high baron.	
RED LION:	By my great god Mohammed,	
	For all the world I will not permit it;	
	She will burn for what has happened	
	Because she accepted your proposal.	

[*Exit all*]

[*Sometime later at the prison*]

GLORIANT: O, almighty King of Heaven,
Now save that noble lady;
Even if I lose my life, 830
Save the beautiful Florentijn,
This I pray you, my true creator!
Let her avoid death
And become a Christian,
This I pray you, Mother and Maid,
For she bears a pure heart
And has a completely noble nature,
Mother of God, protect this beautiful creature!
This I pray you, God, through your mercy,
For true love has put us both 840
In this torment.
O God, do not forget
That love moved you so
That from a vine branch you
Took human form,
It was Mary, the Virgin pure,
Who received your life
(Which has never happened to any other woman)
And as a virgin, brought you into the world.
All this was done by the power of love, 850
And thereafter, you died a bitter death
To bring us into eternal bliss,
In this way, deliver me from this prison.

[*In* FLORENTIJN's *cell sometime later*]

FLORENTIJN: Where are you, Rogier, courageous hero,
My dear and trusted friend?
ROGIER: I am here, truly noble lady.
Now tell me, what can I do for you?
FLORENTIJN: O Rogier, my hope
Lies entirely with you.
O dear Rogier, now tell me, 860

	What does my father say, that high baron?	
ROGIER:	O noble lady, by Mohammed	
	He swears by his teeth[11]	
	That he will hang the great hero	
	And deliver you up to the fire.	
	He has sworn it resolutely,	
	And he will keep his oath, you can be sure.	
	Therefore, noble lady,	
	Sorrow plagues me, every hour, night and day.	
FLORENTIJN:	O noble Rogier, now be trustworthy	870
	For you do have power.	
	I know you guard the prison	
	Where the duke is kept.	
	Now help him	
	So that he may preserve his life.	
ROGIER:	O noble and chosen lady,	
	If I do that, I am dead.	
	All the red gold in the world	
	Would not be able to help me then.	
FLORENTIJN:	O Rogier, please, help me out of my misery	880
	And help the duke, Gloriant.	
	Then we will quit Abelant	
	And escape to the land of Bruuyswijc.	
	Rogier, believe me truly,	
	I will always be your friend.	
ROGIER:	O noble lady, you truly deserve my help.	
	Once upon a time	
	Your father swore that I should die,	
	At that time you were my only hope.	
	Ah, I would be ungrateful	890
	To forget all that.	
	Even if they quarter me for it	
	I will help you, noble lady,	
	So that you will preserve your life	
	And also the Duke of Bruuyswijc,	
	For he received me so warmly	

When I brought him your message.[12]
Even if I should suffer for it day and night,
Noble lady of a pure heart,
I will unlock the stone prison 900
And release the great hero.

[*Sometime later at the prison*[13]]

Where are you, lord Gloriant,
Noble duke, great baron?
Come out of this heavy prison
For all the locks have been opened.

GLORIANT: Who has done me this service?
Rogier friend, tell me that.

ROGIER: Florentijn bid me
To help you in your misery.

GLORIANT: O God, who let himself be crucified, 910
You deserve praise and thanks,
That I have gotten away from this terrible stench
Where I have languished for so long.
Now tell me, where is Florentijn,
That too beautiful creature?

ROGIER: O noble lord, she lies between four walls
Locked up and fast imprisoned.
No one may go to her
Because her father wants to take her life.

GLORIANT: That desire shall not be fulfilled. 920
If God protects my life,
I will release that noble lady
Before I part from here.
O, if I only had my war horse,
Valentine, at hand,
And my sword, the good brand,
Then I could get Florentijn
And pay the Red Lion
His rent in full!
I will make him rue the day 930

GLORIANT

	He put me in this prison to suffer.	
ROGIER:	Lord, I want to help you	
	And leave this country with you.	
	I want to punish Mohammed	
	And become a Christian.	
	Now look, high-born man, here is	
	Valentine, your good horse,	
	And your brand, your good sword,	
	On which your heart is set.	
GLORIANT:	Now I have all I want,	940
	Now, if only I had Florentijn the beautiful!	
	Dear Rogier, God reward you!	
	Now show me the stone prison	
	Where that pure maid lies.	
	I will unlock it,	
	And if the Red Lion notices	
	Then I will give him his reward.	
ROGIER:	O lord, then we will surely be lost	
	For the entire court will hear us.	
	Let me suggest another course:	950
	You stay here in this forest	
	And I shall go to the Red Lion	
	And I shall tell him and advise him	
	That tomorrow with no delay,	
	Florentijn, the noble lady,	
	Should be killed, her life taken,	
	This I will suggest to him.	
	And you will keep yourself here in this forest,	
	Where you must always be on guard.	
	When they bring Florentijn out	960
	And prepare to kill her,	
	Then you must come	
	Riding up, great, high-born hero.	
	By my god Termagant,	
	I will help you!	
	We will attack: you will pierce and I will hit,	

| | And God will be our helper.
| | In this way we will release
| | The noble lady Florentijn.
| GLORIANT: | Rogier, even if it costs me my life   970
| | I will deliver her from this misery.
| | Now go hence and make haste.
| | I shall wait here in the forest.
| | O Father, Son and Holy Ghost,
| | Now you must protect Florentijn!

[*At court*]

| ROGIER: | O Mohammed and Apollo,
| | Mohammed and Termagant,
| | Noble lords of Abelant,
| | I give you good day!
| RED LION: | Rogier, now give me counsel,   980
| | How shall I deal with Gloriant?
| ROGIER: | Noble lord of Abelant,
| | That I will tell you and advise you,
| | Tomorrow without delay,
| | Take Florentijn, that foul woman,
| | And kill her, take her life,
| | For she has truly deserved it,
| | If we judge rightly,
| | For she has blasphemed our god;
| | And you shall take Gloriant   990
| | And hang him from a tree,
| | For if Gheraert his uncle knows
| | That he is imprisoned here,
| | Then he will come with a great might
| | And with all his power
| | He shall make us suffer terribly.
| | Therefore, it seems best to me
| | That you kill both of them.
| RED LION: | Rogier, this advice is sound.
| | I will not wait another hour.   1000

GLORIANT

	Go hence and get me the beautiful lady,
	Florentijn, that foul whore!
	I will take her out of the gates
	And I will have her beheaded.
ROGIER:	Lord, it's best to get it over with.
	I'll go and fetch her, by Apollo!
	[*At* FLORENTIJN's *cell*]
	Where are you, beautiful Florentijn?
	You must go before the high baron,
	Your father, the Red Lion.
	He wants to serve justice 1010
	And means for you to pay the price
	Because you have blasphemed his god
	And because you have slept with
	Gloriant, high and noble lady.
	Because you swore a precious oath to him,
	It will cost you your noble life.
	[*At the place of Execution*]
FLORENTIJN:	God, who was born of a Virgin
	And who suckled her for food,
	And then patiently endured
	Being taken by the foul Jews 1020
	And hung on a cross
	On which he died a bitter death
	To bring us everlasting bliss,
	Have mercy on my soul.
RED LION:	Now tell me, daughter Florentijn,
	Who has taught you this,
	To think like this,
	To pray to a strange god
	And blaspheme our god?
	And further, to love a Christian? 1030
	By my god Termagant,
	You will lose your life for it!
FLORENTIJN:	Father, I gladly choose death,

For the One who died for me
And hanged on a cross naked,
With his arms spread wide,
Who let his hands and his feet be pierced
With three dull nails.
Dear God,
Protect me from the fires of hell, 1040
And save the duke, Gloriant,
For he is in great misery.
O noble, high-born companion,
How much I long to see you!
But it will not happen,
And that pains my heart.

HANGMAN: You will never again see him,
High-born noble lady,
For I shall take your life,
Though it pains my heart. 1050
O noble young lady, Florentijn,
What have you done?
If you pray to Mohammed,
You might still save your life.
It is your fault that all this has happened,
And still you blame our god
And thereby dishonor yourself,
You, who are so high born.

RED LION: You're giving her too long a respite.
Hurry up and cut off her head, 1060
For her crimes are so great,
All the world cannot help her.

[*Enter* GLORIANT *threatening the pagans*]

GLORIANT: By God who let himself be crucified,
That will not be, foul tyrant.
Before God you should be ashamed
Because you are so cruel.
This is a bad time for you, you'd better get out,

	Or the devil will come and get you.	
	Florentijn will keep her life	
	And I will let it be to your shame.	1070
	[*The* RED LION, FLOERANT *and the* HANGMAN *run off*]	
	O dearest Florentijn	
	From this death you are set free!	
	You can thank the worthy Virgin Mary	
	And Rogier, that courageous hero, for your reprise.	
GLORIANT:	O noble duke, Gloriant,	
	I thank God in heaven	
	That it has gone so well for me,	
	And I thank you and Rogier also.	
	O noble lord, let us go away from here	
	Great, high-born man.	1080
GLORIANT:	Florentijn, now let us journey	
	To my country of Bruuyswijc.[14]	
	[*Sometime later at the gates of Bruuyswijc*]	
	My heart is rich in happiness.	
	Noble lady of high birth,	
	Now I see the noble orchard,	
	Bruuyswijc, that good land.	
	O noble uncle, courageous hero	
	Of Normandy, high baron,	
	Now let the gates open wide	
	And let her in with a joyful heart,	1090
	She whom I love with all my heart,	
	The beautiful Florentijn of Abelant.	
GHERAERT:	O Gloriant, my nephew,	
	Be welcome on this day,	
	And Florentijn whom I have never seen	
	Before this time now.	
	My heart overflows with happiness	
	Because I see you are unwounded,	
	Coming with the noble lady.	
	Now tell me, what happened in Abelant?	1100

GLORIANT:	O noble uncle, courageous hero,
	When I was sleeping I was taken prisoner there
	And put in a jail,
	From which I longed to get free,
	For adders, toads and snakes
	Were there my closest neighbors.
	But God protected me, and
	With the help of friends and good advice,
	I came out without injury
	From this terrible prison. 1110
	No one has ever been in such danger.
	But the love of a noble woman
	Kept me alive,
	Hoping that things would get better.
	And so I have with endurance
	Won that which my heart desired.
GHERAERT:	Gloriant, nephew, you have
	Learned to build love's orchard,
	And you must not regret it,
	Even though it was quite painful. 1120
	You bring to us a beautiful creature,
	Who, by the way, could not be more excellent.
	Even though her father is a Saracen,
	He is a high-born man,
	For the Sultan of Babylon
	Was his father, this I know,
	And the daughter of a lord of Antioch
	Was his mother, of this I'm sure.
	Her father is renowned
	In all of Christendom, 1130
	His courage has no equal
	Among any in pagan lands who carry a sword.
	That is why I feared
	That you would come to misfortune.
	But you have done well, and
	By endurance you have won.

> Indeed, it's always better
> To finish what you've started.
> [*Turning to the audience*]
> Now quiet and be still!
> Our play is done.[15]　　　　　　　　　　1140
> Now we will play a farce for you

Notes

[1] The last judgment was to take place in the Valley of Josephat, according to the prophet, Joel (3:2).
[2] A place somewhere in the Near East.
[3] There has been quite some speculation as to what this "portrait" could be. The idea of the likeness being "printed," suggests to some critics that it is literally a portrait, a painting, or a print. But the word, "gheprent," literally "imprinted," had a broader meaning than its literal application suggests. Leendertz proposes, in a lengthy discussion, that it most likely refers to a small (thus portable) sculpture, perhaps of ivory (v. 2, 507–8).
[4] "Hovescheit," means courtly love or courtliness in the service of women.
[5] This sign seems to be a crest or an emblem of a falcon, which is likely borne on his chest or head-dress. At line 625 the image of a falcon trained to hunt is linked to courtly behavior; as the falcon descends on Florentijn's hand, Gloriant comes to take her hand in marriage.
[6] At some point in this exchange, it's not clear where, Floerant, the nephew of the Red Lion, overhears the lovers' conversation.
[7] In other words, Florentijn wants to be sure that Gloriant's intentions toward her are honorable, and further, that he will guard her virginity until they marry.
[8] On horseback, as a knight.
[9] He is not a Moslem.
[10] The allusion to a castle and its castle-keeper is a pun, "casteel," castle, also referring to a lock. Gloriant will be under lock and key, thus he is the lock-keeper.
[11] "By Mohammed's teeth," comes from an incident in the Prophet's life. Mohammed, during a battle, was wounded, his cheek and upper lip were pierced and he lost his front teeth. It is a traditional Moslem oath. Roemans and Gaspar, 53.
[12] The Duke was a good and hospitable host to Rogier.
[13] It is not entirely clear if Gloriant and Florentijn are imprisoned in the same place. At v. 872–3, Florentijn refers to the "prison where the Duke is

kept," as if it's a different place from where she is locked up. She might simply be under guard in the castle, although later, at v. 943–5, Gloriant will say: "show me the stone prison/ Where that pure maid lies./ I will unlock it." Clearly, we are meant to think that the lovers are suffering and imprisoned apart from one another and that Rogier must prove himself the faithful servant, and once again, act as their go-between.

14   Here they depart to arrive in Bruuyswijc in the next lines.
15   Again, as at the end of *Lanseloet* (952–5), the line reads, the first play or first part of the performance is done.

P. Bruegel, "Two Peasants." Cleveland Museum of Art.

The Box-Blower
"De Buskenblaser"

Dramatis Personae

The FIRST MAN
His WIFE
The SECOND MAN, called, the other man
The neighbor, GHEERT

FIRST MAN [*to the audience*]: Look at me, I'm standing
                                  right here!
I mill wheat and love to drink beer.
Purses and gloves I can sew,
Hay and corn I can mow.
Yes, and if I wanted,
I'd be good at buying and selling.
I'm a carpenter too
But it doesn't do much for me.
I'm a miller and I know how to mill,
I'm quick to borrow, slow to pay up. 10
I can row and chop,
I can brew and bake.
Dams and dikes both can I make,
I can thresh the chaff from the grain.
And I can do a lot more.
Say, is there a woman or a man here
Who'd like to hire me as their servant?
Even though I like to sleep late?
Even though I'm not a hard worker?
Is there perhaps someone who sees something 20
                                  in me,

                    Who'd like to hire me as his man?
                    I can do a good job at dinner,
                    And I can dig a fine hole for you.
SECOND MAN [*coming in*]: Well, I can fix stone pots
                    And milk pails turned out of clay.
FIRST MAN   [*indignant*]: Surely the devil must have brought
                                                         you blowing in,
                    Cracking your jokes.
SECOND MAN: God give you a cramp in your jaw!
                    You think I'm joking?
                    I want to earn my bread just as much as you,   30
                    For I have a wife and children at home.
FIRST MAN: Yeah, sure. Sounds pretty stupid to me,
                    Repairing stone pots and milk pails!
                    If you can put 'em together again,
                    You're a better man than I!
SECOND MAN: Do you think that's all I can do?
                    Well, if I wanted to make the effort
                    To dig in my bag of tricks,
                    I could turn you into a horse,
                    Worth, I'd say, about ten pounds,   40
                    With black hair and woolly too.
FIRST MAN   [*changing his tone*]: Why then, God must have
                                                          sent you to me
                    For I see that you are a magician!
                    If you could only get rid of my gray hair
                    And make me ten years younger,
                    Then my wife would like me again and
                    I'd give you a big tip.
SECOND MAN: Sure, I can do that. I can make you so gorgeous
                    That you'll drive your wife crazy.
                    If you'll just blow into this little box,   50
                    You'll quickly turn another color,
                    You'll change so much
                    That your wife will hardly recognize you.
FIRST MAN: On my word, if this works

                    You'll be rewarded.
SECOND MAN: By God, when you go home to her
                    Your wife will surely notice.
FIRST MAN: Then even if it costs me a pretty penny,
                    I'll never be pushed around again.
                    She teases me all the time just because I'm ugly. 60
                    I can't live in peace!
                    Here you go, look what I'll give you,
                    This fine purse with money in it too.
                    Yesterday, I sold my good cow,
                    She sold for forty pounds and ten shillings —
                    There's all the money I got for her,
                    You can have it all for yourself.
SECOND MAN: Here, put this little box to your lips
                    And blow in it as hard as you can.
                    I have conjured some powerful magic —   70
                    It's sure to work!
FIRST MAN: But will it help my singing too?
                    Because I'm not good at that either.
SECOND MAN: Sure! Your hair will lose its gray
                    And your voice will become clear.
FIRST MAN: Wow, God grant you a good year!
                    Beside my money, receive my thanks too.
                    If I can sing better to boot
                    Then it's surely money well spent.
SECOND MAN: Blow into the box, for God who knows all. . . .   80
                    [*First man blows*] Good goin', m'boy, now
                                                                    you're a man!
                    I swear to you by St. John,
                    That no one who knew you before,
                    No one in the world,
                    Will recognize you now!
FIRST MAN: Now God and a little luck will decide
                    How I fare with my wife,
                    Who has complained about my ugliness now
                    For four days and five.

	I want to go home right away,	90
	And let her see how attractive I've become.	
	She has complained so much	
	That I am ugly and old,	
	Now she can't fault me there	
	For my face has another skin.	
SECOND MAN:	You're right about that.	
	[*aside*] And the cash cow is in the bank!	
	[*Sometime later outside his house*]	
FIRST MAN	[*leaping in the air*]: Hey, look, I can even	
	jump better.	
	[*singing a tune*] By God, look how well I can sing!	
	Praise and thanks to God,	
	My voice is so much better,	100
	I'm a newborn beauty!	
	O wife, my sweetie pie, let me in,	
	And come and take a look at me.	
	[*She comes to the door*]	
WIFE:	Christ, stop making such a racket!	
	What the devil, who got a hold of you?	
FIRST MAN:	I have bathed in the fountain of youth,	
	Aren't you a little interested in me now?	
	My beauty has cost me plenty,	
	The whole price of our cow.	
WIFE:	Thanks to the devil, I'm sure,	110
	You gave away our money for that?	
FIRST MAN:	Yes, I've got nothing left.	
	I even let him keep the purse.	
	He put a little box to my lips	
	Into which I blew with all my might,	
	And out of it came such a force	
	That made me into the beautiful creature	
	you see before you.	
WIFE:	Christ! Get out of here, God have mercy on you,	
	A woman is cursed with a husband like this!	

THE BOX-BLOWER 151

	It must have been the devil brought us together.	120
	You're as black as a moor!	
FIRST MAN:	What the devil! What do you take me for?	
	Isn't my voice sweet? Am I not beautiful	
	and fair?	
WIFE:	Sure you are, like a bad dream!	
	I never saw an uglier creature.	
	Hey, Gheert, dear neighbor,	
	Come and look at my husband!	
	[*Enter* GHEERT]	
GHEERT:	What Goesen,[1] by St. John,	
	Who did that to you?	
	You must have taken a dip in a tub of paint,[2]	130
	Your face is covered in black.	
FIRST MAN:	Oh no, did I get taken again?	
	Is it true?	
	Let me look in a good mirror,	
	So I can see myself.	
WIFE:	No problem, we can arrange that!	
FIRST MAN	[*looking into the mirror*]: Jesus Christ!	
	Help, good people!	
	I have never seen anything so monstrous,	
	Never was a man so deceived!	
WIFE:	And you thought I was lying,	140
	You dirty mean old sot!	
FIRST MAN:	No, you speak the truth, so help me God,	
	I am the fool now.	
	My dearest sweetheart,	
	Help me, I have to get rid of it.	
WIFE:	By God, I don't give a damn,	
	If you look like that forever.	
FIRST MAN:	I know, you don't care	
	If my face is screwed up.	
	Good neighbor, good Gheert,	150
	How will I get rid of this?	

GHEERT:	Maybe you should dunk your face in piss and mud And stuff like that.³
FIRST MAN:	No, No! I'll gag If you dunk me in stale piss.
WIFE:	I wish I had the money from my cow, The money you spent so easily! And I wish that you had taken a dip in a shit hole, Dirty, old, creep!
FIRST MAN:	Even if it made you twice as mad, my wife, 160 And even if you'd scream at me for it, I'd put the money for our pig down right now If only I could be rid of this mess.
WIFE:	Christ! Get out of here! [*to the whole neighborhood*] Come and see How handsome my husband has become!
FIRST MAN:	That bum told me I'd be handsome and learn to sing, That I'd be young and be able to jump miles, And that you'd be very pleased with me! 170
GHEERT:	By God, let's give him the benefit of the doubt, He meant to do good.
WIFE:	Christ! Get out, good neighbor, and shut up! You're driving me crazy too! He deserves a smack on the jaw And I wish he'd never come to my house again.
FIRST MAN:	Shut up, in the devil's name, You didn't hear me make such a fuss When you took the money from our dappled cow And blew it on a lollard brother. 180 You even gave him my good gray jacket As a guarantee for his expenses. I'll tell you even if it's embarassing, I'll even tell it to all the neighbors!
GHEERT:	Hey neighbor, shut your mouth

The Box-Blower

	Or you'll dishonor your wife.	
WIFE:	God give him a cramp in his cheek,	
	How could he say that about me?	
FIRST MAN:	I saw the scum-bag lying on top of you	
	I saw him with his tenderloin up your ass,	190
	And he lay flat out, not sideways,	
	I saw it really well, what you two did.	
	And since then, when I saw you with your knees bare,	
	I haven't been the same.	
WIFE:	Maybe I was looking for fleas,	
	You dirty old geezer!	
FIRST MAN:	What the devil was the lollard doing,	
	That he lay pumping up and down?	
WIFE:	God damn you for the foul bastard you are,	
	We had a pretty good time of it!	200
FIRST MAN:	O yeah? Well it didn't do much	
	For me, your little game.	
WIFE:	Shut up! I wish you were dead,	
	You old sleaze bag!	
	I'll bash your teeth in!	

They fight[4]

Good people, this play is over;[5]
You can all go home
By the ladder below.
And if it pleases you, come again.   210

NOTES

[1] Goeson (Gosewijn) the "one man's" name, as in *Rubben*, is a traditional name meaning God's son, that is, Everyman.
[2] "Weedcupe," literally a "weed-cup," "weed" being the name of a plant from which blue dye and paint were made.
[3] Wool was prepared and cleaned by cloth makers in a mud bath mixture of urine and clay.
[4] Original rubric.
[5] It's not clear who the speaker is.

"Lanseloet courts Sanderijn," *Lanseloet van Denemarken*. Gouda: Govert van Ghemen, ca. 1486–92.

LANSELOET

The abel spel of Lanseloet of Denmark,
how he loved a young lady who served his mother[1]
and the farce which follows it.

Dramatis Personae

LANSELOET of Denmark

Lanseloet's MOTHER

SANDERIJN, a young lady serving the mother of Lanseloet

REINHOUT, a friend and vassal of Lanseloet

A KNIGHT

THE KNIGHT'S FORESTER

PROLOGUE

> I pray to God in heaven
> And to Mary, the beautiful virgin,
> That they protect us all
> And keep us virtuous
> So that we will reach the kingdom of heaven.
> This I pray to the Virgin Mary, the queen,
> Who is a woman above all.[2]
> Now hear what we shall put on for you.
> It is mostly about a knight
> Who loved an excellent young lady.   10
> She was fine-hearted, courteous and pure,
> But in wealth and also in birth

She was beneath him.
His mother was enraged
That he could put his love so low,
But his heart leapt with joy
Whenever he saw her noble person.
His mother, that cruel creature,
Grew indignant and bitter.
She warned him now and again   20
That he was stooping too low.
But he argued in return
With the most courteous words he could find.
And always he drew closer to her,
This beautiful lady, called Sanderijn,
Who could not have been more excellent,
Even though she was born too low for him.
But Lanseloet's love made his mother spiteful
And ultimately, she destroyed it.
Now I ask that you mark it,   30
Pay attention and weigh it, for
I believe that you never have
Heard or seen a love like this.
Now I ask you, poor and rich,
To be quiet to the end.
Now mark how it begins.

[*Denmark, in an orchard*]

LANSELOET: O, Lord God, how can it be
I love the sweet Sanderijn;
I have completely lost my heart to her,
Even though every day   40
I've been warned against it by my mother.
I must hear many bitter words
Because I love beneath my station.
Still, love has so pierced me
That I cannot turn away from her.
Whenever I catch a glimpse of her

LANSELOET

	I want to speak to her.	
	But it grieves my mother so	
	That I must hide how I feel.	
	I will wait here for my beloved	50
	Under this eglantine	
	Because I know she will come	
	To this orchard.	
SANDERIJN	[*entering*]: O noble knight of high birth,	
	God, who is more powerful than all things,	
	Grant you a good day,	
	Noble knight of the free heart.	
LANSELOET:	O beautiful maid, God who is with us,	
	Keep us virtuous and	
	Protect us from all things evil,	60
	Especially from jealous tongues,	
	So that nothing will be said	
	About either of us that is malicious.	
	O Sanderijn, give me your advice.	
	My heart is twisted out of joint	
	And pines for your love.	
	O Sanderijn, truly beautiful maid,	
	If I cannot have you as my wife,	
	I will die;	
	It will cost me my life	70
	And I will be lost for all eternity.	
SANDERIJN:	O, noble, high-born knight,	
	That may never happen.	
	Even though I am happy to see you,	
	Noble knight, I am not your equal,	
	You are too great and too rich	
	For me ever to be your wife.	
	That's why it must be like this and remain so,	
	And even if I love you in my heart	
	I cannot simply become your lover	80
	Because there is no man who lives under	
	heaven's vault,	

| | Even if he were a king and wore a crown,
| | For whom I'd give up my virginity.
| LANSELOET: | O, beautiful maid of a pure heart,
| | If you would do my bidding,
| | My dearest Sanderijn,
| | You would not be unrewarded.
| | Strange things can happen and
| | You still might become my wife.
| | Have mercy on me and be true,   90
| | Come with me into the castle,
| | I shall give you a jewel,
| | Whose like, I think, you have never seen.
| SANDERIJN: | No, noble lord, I am still a virgin.
| | For this I thank God in heaven.
| | Even if you gave me a gift of
| | A thousand marcs of red gold,
| | High baron, noble friend,
| | Even so, Lanseloet, high-born lord,
| | I would still choose to keep   100
| | Myself chaste. I may not be rich in goods,
| | Nor descended from a high family,
| | But still I mean to keep my maidenhead.
| | I will not be known
| | As any man's lover, Lord Lanseloet,
| | For I want to love honorably
| | And without shame.
| LANSELOET: | Sanderijn, by the Virgin Mary,
| | Shame is not what lies ahead of you.
| | There is no woman born   110
| | On earth, under heaven's vault,
| | So rich, so great, or so beautiful,
| | Who will make me as fortunate as you.
| | O Sanderijn, will you then
| | Leave me to languish in this sorrow?
| | And in this condition
| | Should I not receive your pity?

	Come and play in the woods	
	Here, in this green valley,	
	Where the little birds are singing,	120
	And the flowers are growing amid the green;	
	Beautiful maid, there will be no wrongdoing,	
	Everything will be honorable.	
SANDERIJN:	Lord Lanseloet, it is often said:	
	"With little faith, many are deceived."³	
	This is surely true and not a lie.	
	For it is everywhere to be seen,	
	Women are treated unfairly	
	Because they trust men too much,	
	And when everything is said and done	130
	They always come to regret it.	
	I know no one born on earth	
	Whom I would trust that,	
	If I went to play with him in the forest,	
	He would not do with me whatever he liked.	
LANSELOET:	But I love you too much	
	To dishonor your body,	
	Sanderijn, truly beautiful maid.	
	Even if I had the opportunity, beautiful maid,	
	It is not my intention.	140
	I would not want to cause you any shame.	
	If we were in a strange country,	
	Sanderijn, my dearest one,	
	I would myself go and beg for your bread	
	Rather than let you go hungry.	
	On my knighthood, I would not harm you,	
	I would do nothing Sanderijn, against your will.	
SANDERIJN:	Lord Lanseloet, we've been here too long;	
	Someone might hear or see us,	
	For slanderers are always looking for	150
	an opportunity	
	To catch someone in a scandal.	
	And stool pigeons rather sing of bad	

	Than good, for it is their nature.	
	Now let us part quickly,	
	So that no one takes notice of us.	
	High baron, noble friend,	
	God our Lord preserve you,	
	And always keep you in virtue	
	Wherever you go.	

[*Exit* SANDERIJN]

LANSELOET:	O how the beautiful Sanderijn	160
	Has wounded my heart!	
	She does not want to do what I want	
	And so I'm made to suffer.	
	No matter how I wail, how I protest,	
	She will not go with me into the forest.	
	Because she loves honor above gold,	
	That I know from what she has said.	
	She is chaste and pure	
	And her heart is wholly noble.	
	By my knighthood, I know for certain,	170
	That if she was born my equal,	
	Even if she were not rich in goods,	
	I would make her my wife.	
	But she will not give herself to me	
	She guards her chastity with care;	
	Her heart is honorable	
	And therefore my heart languishes in sorrow.	

[*Enter Lanseloet's* MOTHER *from a hiding place on stage*]

MOTHER:	Lanseloet of Denmark,	
	I overheard your love making!	
	Lanseloet, by the Virgin Mary,	180
	I can't believe what's going on,	
	Why don't you consider your worth more seriously?	
	How can you give your love away so easily?	
	Besides it's unmanly to cry!	

	That one doesn't even care for you!	
	You're a disgrace,	
	Loving a woman so beneath you!	
LANSELOET:	O mother, she is so pure,	
	And her heart is so honest,	
	And her ways so noble,	190
	That I am doomed to love her always.	
	My heart burns and blazes	
	When I see her.	
	Dear mother, noble woman,	
	Whatever happens I must love her.	
MOTHER:	Lanseloet, I want you to remember who you are,	
	Your noble person and your high birth,	
	Listen to my advice	
	And love an equal.	
LANSELOET:	I know no woman in all of Christendom	200
	Whom I would rather have than Sanderijn.	
	With your permission, dear mother,	
	I wish she could be mine.	
	Certainly, if the whole world were mine to command,	
	I would want her as my wife.	
MOTHER:	Aren't you ashamed of the disgrace, you foolish wretch,	
	Loving so beneath you,	
	While there are so many beautiful young ladies	
	Of high birth and great wealth available.	
LANSELOET:	O dear mother, the power of love	210
	Sees not high birth nor worldly wealth	
	But seeks her equal in spirit.[4]	
	Love understands that "these two are of one mind."	
	I have often heard it read	
	That love seeks her equal	
	Even if one is poor and the other rich.	
	Noble love does her work.	

	True love does not give up,
	Not to riches, nor to greatness of degree.
	Love does not at any time nor in any day 220
	diminish,
	It comes by chance.
	Give noble love her due for
	She does not see such things as high birth.
MOTHER:	O Lanseloet, I see how obsessed
	Your heart is with Sanderijn.
	All right then, follow my plan and
	I will get you what you want.
	Tonight, all night, secretly and quietly,
	Lord knight, stay in your room,
	And you will be able to do all you desire 230
	But you must promise me one thing. . . .
LANSELOET:	Lady, mother, by Saint Simeon,
	Whatever you wish I will promise
	As long as I can feast with her[5]
	In my room, just us two, alone together.
MOTHER:	Lanseloet, promise me,
	On your loyalty to your knighthood
	That you, when you have finished
	with the young lady, Sanderijn,
	When you have done all you like with her,
	That you will say, "I have had enough, 240
	Sanderijn, I'm stuffed,
	I've gorged myself
	As if I'd eaten seven slabs of bacon."
	This, you must not forget,
	And these are exactly the words you must speak.
	Then you must turn away from her for
	the entire night,
	And lie and sleep sweetly and softly,
	Without saying a single word more.
LANSELOET:	O dear mother, is it your will that
	I say such beastly things? 250

LANSELOET

                The like of which I have never heard. . . .
                How can this help you?
                If I should take these words
                And say them to Sanderijn
                And then lie there like a stinking dog,
                A villain, what would that pure maid think
                If I said nothing else?
                I, who at first treated her so well,
                And then put her to shame?
                Her thoughts would pierce my heart.   260
MOTHER: Lanseloet, this is what I require:
                If you want her in your power,
                Then you must promise me this,
                And keep your word as an honorable man.
LANSELOET: Lady mother, bring her to me
                And I shall do as you wish,
                Even if it breaks my heart.

                [*Exit Lanseloet's* MOTHER]

LANSELOET [*alone*]: Many men say things they don't mean.
                I'll be the same as everyone else;
                Whatever words my mouth utters   270
                I will not mean in my heart,
                For I wish her every good.
                I pray God, the lord of all,
                That she will not hold this against me, for
                She is so pious and so good that,
                If she takes it wrongly,
                Her heart will become a stranger to me,
                And then my heart will live in torment forever.

                [*Exit* LANSELOET, *enter his* MOTHER]

MOTHER: And now I have done everything
                I need to part those two.   280
                He does not know how to behave.
                He, the noblest knight of our land,
                Wants to disgrace himself completely.

He loves this lowly woman,
And for certain that he would marry her
If I let him, foolish wretch.
But I will arrange things differently,
It will never be. . . .
Where are you beautiful maid, Sanderijn?
Come quickly, I must speak with you. 290

[*Enter* SANDERIJN]

SANDERIJN: High born lady that you are,
Now tell me, what is your wish?
MOTHER: Sanderijn I must tell you
Something which distresses my heart.
My dear son Lanseloet
Has fallen sick.
Last night he fell so ill
That he could not speak a word.
I don't know what's the matter with him,
Or what makes him suffer, 300
But this morning, when it was light,
He made a great sigh.
Sanderijn, I fear for his life;
My heart aches for him.
Now I beg you, beautiful maid, Sanderijn,
Go to Lanseloet.
He is in great need.
My heart is overwhelmed with grief.
SANDERIJN: O noble lady, I am pleased to do
What you ask of me and 310
I will gladly go with you,
For if anything happens to him,
                    it would pain me greatly.
MOTHER [*aside*]: It pays to keep your eyes open
If you want to live honorably!
Yes, this is how one lays the trap
To catch a woman in a snare,

"Lanseloet's mother tricks Sanderijn," *Lanseloet van Denemarken*. Gouda: Govert van Ghemen, ca. 1486–92.

And who could do it better than I?
I know that when his desire is quenched
His love will pale,
It always happens this way. 320

[*Sometime later*]

Now she has been with him in the room.[6]

SANDERIJN: O God, who suffered on the cross,
How could his mother be so cruel?
I now understand much more
Than I did yesterday evening.
She told me a pretty lie, saying
That he was taken ill,
That's how she led me into the snare.
By telling me lies for truth
She brought me under Lanseloet's power, 330
Which I shall always regret.
But what hurt me above everything else
Were the words that the free knight spoke
When he turned his face away from me
As if I were a stinking dog!
These lie buried in my heart,
They torment me in the depths of my being.
I want never again for him
To know anything about me, good or bad.
I shall leave and go my own way, 340
To wander in strange lands.
I pray God to hide the disgrace
Which has been forced on me,
For it was done without gratitude—
This is too much for me.
Lanseloet, you will never see me again.

[SANDERIJN *walking along, coming to a forest*]

I will mourn here in the forest,
O Father, Son and Holy Ghost,

LANSELOET

              I ask you to spare my life,
              And vouchsafe that I'll never again have to   350
              Be ashamed to act as any man's wife.
              Whatever country I go to,
              Let me remain as I am.
              I pray to the mother and the free maid,
              Fountain of purity,
              That shame will never again
              Be brought to me by a man.
              This I pray you, fountain flowing in virtue,
              Worthy mother and virgin pure.
              I see ahead a beautiful fountain,[7]   360
              There I will take my rest.
              I have been fasting for such a long time
              That I am hungry and thirsty.
              I must have something to drink, for
              I can bear it no longer.

    [SANDERIJN *goes to the fountain; meantime, enter a* KNIGHT]

KNIGHT: Now, God willing, I'll go to the hunt.
              I pray to God in heaven
              And Mary, the beautiful virgin,
              To protect me
              And bless me and make me lucky   370
              So that when I hunt, I'll catch something
              Because it's been a long time since
                            I've caught anything.
              Really, I'm mortified . . .
              It's been four days now
              And I haven't caught so much as a rabbit.
              My heart is perplexed!
              I've tried so hard and I've come up with nothing!
              Let me sound my horn,
              And see if God will help me.
              Now he sounds his horn[8]   380
              By the lord who made me

I see in the distance the game
My heart desires most.
I think no one on any other day
Has seen such perfect game as this.
In the distance, I think I see
A maiden, beautiful and pure,
Sitting by a fountain.
O God, how will I catch her?
I better not waste any time. 390
I will sound my horn again
And see what she does.

Again he sounds his horn

O, God, who is lord above all,
You must give me the chance
To convince this beautiful creature
To love me.

[*Approaching* SANDERIJN]

O, beautiful maid, don't move:
I must have you!
I'd rather capture you than a wild boar 400
Made of finely wrought gold.
I thank God for this perfect hunt
And that I rose with dawn this morning to see it!

SANDERIJN: O noble and excellent knight,
Please don't disgrace me.
This I ask you on your nobility.
Do not do anything to dishonor me
Because it will cause you great shame
When you appear at court.
You seem to me to be a knight 410
                  of great reputation,
That's why I pray you, noble baron,
Do nothing to harm me,
Please leave me just as I am.

KNIGHT: O beautiful maid, now tell me,

"Sanderijn meets the Knight," *Lanseloet van Denemarken*. Gouda: Govert van Ghemen, ca. 1486–92.

How did you come to this forest?
It astonishes me
To find you alone like this,
Here by this fountain.
What has happened to you?
Has someone planned a rendezvous with you,　420
That you await, beautiful maid?
He's probably of such a high rank
That I shouldn't even be speaking to you.

SANDERIJN: O noble knight, for no man
Do I wait here, noble baron,
There are other reasons why I'm here.
I am forlorn. From my home,
Where I lived happily and respected,
I am lost, I know not where.
I am here full of dread and　430
I don't know where I shall go.
I lament to God, it is my misfortune
To know the bitterness of life.

KNIGHT: Still I thank God for my fortune:
I rose with the dawn this morning
And on my hunt I found
Such a noble beauty!
God has brought us together,
Of that I am certain.
You were made for me to love　440
For you please me in everything;
Your beauty, your courtly language,
Everything about you pleases me.
We will have great feasting together![9]
Now come with me to my castle,
And you will never see a jewel so beautiful
As the one that will be yours and mine.

SANDERIJN: Lord knight, leave off your tale for a moment.
I pray to God the almighty,
That you must not taunt me　450

	Even though I am forlorn.	
KNIGHT:	O beautiful maid, my whole heart is burning
	With the fire of love.
	You are so refined and so perfect
	That I swear on my knighthood, you shall be
	my wife,
	For you are so noble and so beautiful,
	But take my offer only if your will desires it.
	I beg you, tell me your name, for truly,
	You must be my wife.
SANDERIJN:	O noble knight, are you earnest?	460
	My name I will gladly tell you.
	I am called Sanderijn
	And my father was called Robbrecht.
	He was well-born, a knight-at-arms,
	Who served the King of Auvergne.
KNIGHT:	O, beautiful maid, I am glad to hear
	That you descend from a noble family.
	And again I thank God for the great good luck,
	That this morning I rose with the dawn.
	It was an angel who called me	470
	To come to the woods and hunt.
	My eyes have never seen a more beautiful
	woman.
	Truly you will be mine!
SANDERIJN:	Lord knight, if it is to be
	Then I will gladly give myself to you,
	And thank God and you for this honor,
	Because you would love beneath your station.
	You have been so kind to me,
	Speaking with noble and beautiful words.
	I pray God that he reward you,	480
	For your heart is noble
	To speak to me so kindly
	In this place.
KNIGHT:	O beautiful maid, let us go then!

SANDERIJN:	I give you my holy promise as my guarantee. But first, let us go into this garden, Lord knight, to speak a little, And please understand my reasoning, This I pray you, high-born baron.	
	[*In the garden*]	
	Here is a tree, beautiful and green,	490
	Full of gorgeous blossoms.	
	Its noble fragrance spreads	
	Throughout the orchard.	
	It grows in a rich valley	
	And, therefore, it has many blooms.	
	It is so noble and so sweet	
	That it adorns the entire orchard.	
	Suppose now that a high-born falcon	
	Flew onto this tree and dallied here,	
	And then took a blossom from the tree,	500
	And then nevermore returned,	
	Never again and never touched the tree again,	
	Should the tree then be hated ever after	
	And should it be felled and deserted?	
	This I pray you tell me,	
	Speak the just truth,	
	Noble knight, in courteous fashion.	
KNIGHT:	Noble woman, I understand you exactly;	
	One flower is nothing,	
	So long as no others will be taken—	510
	For this I cannot possibly hate the tree.	
	Nor fell it, nor desert it,	
	For it grows so beautifully.	
	I see so many flowers blooming on this tree	
	In great bunches, impossible to count,	
	Which will produce noble fruit,	
	If God will permit it.	
	From now on, no more talk of this,	

LANSELOET

Come with me, truly beautiful wife.

[Exit SANDERIJN and the KNIGHT]

[Meanwhile, in Denmark]

LANSELOET: By my faith, all the pleasures of the world 520
Are gone.
I cannot find her anywhere,
O most beautiful Sanderijn!
I have my mother to thank
For giving me those cruel words.
I thought my heart would break
When I spoke them.
That's why she has stolen away from me
And run off quietly.
This is my mother's doing, 530
She, who made me speak those words.
Until I see my noble woman,
I will never have peace again.
I love her beautiful body
So much that I think I will dissolve from grief.
To be with her is to be alive
Because she is so excellent.
She is a woman of the highest order,
The empress of my five senses.
There is no man who could love a woman more 540
Than I love her, nor no one who could love her
                                          as well.
I shall look all over Christendom,
Until I know where she is.
Where are you Reinhout? Come to me,
My oldest and best friend.

REINHOUT: *[entering]*: O noble lord, why is it
That you are so forlorn?

LANSELOET: O me, I never thought I'd suffer as much
As I have these last hours,
Since I have lost 550

That noble creature, Sanderijn.
I think my heart will break
Under the great sorrow I must bear.
It is a miracle I haven't
Lost my mind.
I would rather be dead
Than never to see her again!
Reinhout, you must go and search,
See if you can find her,
For I will never be happy 560
Unless I behold her with my own eyes.
Reinhout, my trust is in you.
Go and look for her, go east and south,
And tell her I will make her my bride
In spite of my family.

REINHOUT: Lord, I will gladly risk
My life and I will spare no labor.
But perhaps it is better to let it go —
It's not clear how she will react.

LANSELOET: O Reinhout, her heart is full of honor 570
And her body is so pure
I know that she would not lower herself
For all the riches in the world.
This I know truly,
Her mind is noble.
Reinhout, go as fast as you can,
And look for her everywhere,
In the east and the north, the south, the west,
Until you find her,
For my heart truly loves her, 580
My eyes never saw a dearer woman.

[*Sometime later, in the forest of the* KNIGHT's *castle*]

THE KNIGHT'S FORESTER: I'm right, it's not fair!
For many years
I have wandered here and there

"The Knight's Forester," Flemish or German. Early sixteenth century. The Wallace Collection, Hertford House, London.

As my lord's forester
Guarding his woods
And the fountain in his forest.
Often, days and hours at a time,
I have walked along this riverbank,
But never has the good luck come my way   590
To meet a woman —
I am justified in this complaint —
Never did I meet even one!
But yesterday, when my lord got up
And decided to go out for a hunt . . .
Well, I'm sure my eyes have never seen
A more beautiful woman than the one he found.
He took her courteously by the hand
And brought her to the court full of joy.
If she had been an empress   600
She could not have been more excellent.
She is called Sanderijn
And he has made her his wife.
Still, I'm sorry that
It's never happened to me!
By God, I'm going to have a look around
Every day, morning, noon and night. . . .
If I could catch a ruby-lipped beauty like that,
I'd be pretty happy,
And I would thank God with my all my heart   610
Each and every day.
Now I will hide myself behind this bush
And wait for my chance.

    [*Enter* REINHOUT]

REINHOUT: Maria, mother and virgin pure,
I ask you to guide me
And to give me true and good news
About the one called Sanderijn
Because the heart of Lanseloet, my lord,

Is twisted out of joint.
He pines for her love, 620
He cannot endure his sorrow,
For he has lost his heart and
And all his joy.
He has sworn on his knighthood
That if I can find her, he will make her his wife.
His remorse is great because
He lost her.
He lives in great torment.
All this because of true love.
O Lord God, if I could bring her to him 630
I would be over-joyed. . . .

   [REINHOUT *noticing* THE FORESTER]

Lord God, who will tell me
What that man wants, the one standing
                            over there?
He seems to have an ominous manner,
And he carries a big, heavy club,
He's probably a villain,
Or maybe not . . . ?
Still, I'll ride up to him,
There seems to be only one man and
I never met a lone man 640
Who could frighten me.

   [REINHOUT *approaching* THE FORESTER]

Friend, God grant you good day,
And a happy morning.
May God give good health
To you in all times!

THE KNIGHT'S FORESTER: Friend, God save you. Who are you
That you speak to me so warmly?
REINHOUT: Now tell me, my good man,
Have you at any time seen a servant girl
                            pass by here,

	One who is beautiful and courtly?	650
THE KNIGHT'S FORESTER:	Friend, let me tell you,
	I have wandered here many days,
	And truly I never saw a woman,
	Young or old.
	But about a year ago,[10]
	My lord the good knight
	Got up one morning
	To hunt, and he came to this fountain.
	Here he found hidden
	A pure-hearted servant-girl.	660
	He gladly brought her home as his catch
	And called out that he had hunted well
	Because he brought as his game a maid
	Who was beautiful and well-born.
REINHOUT:	Friend, I must know more about this;
	What was her name?
THE KNIGHT'S FORESTER:	Friend, I will tell you the truth;
	Her name is Sanderijn.
	And she could not be more refined
	Or more well-fashioned.	670
	No woman in this country
	Is her equal.
	She is beautiful and good as well.
	He has made her his wife
	Because she is so dear to him,
	So obedient and so humble.
	And all the kin of my lord
	Love her for her great virtue;
	And all those who belong to the court
	Are improved by her presence.	680
REINHOUT:	Now God stand by me!
	This is the damsel I mean,
	I have sought this pure woman
	For many miles and through many lands,
	But never did I come where I found

	Such good news as you now give me.	
	O dear friend, give me some advice,	
	How will I be able to talk to her?	
THE KNIGHT'S FORESTER:	Friend, you can forget about	
	Speaking to my lady,	690
	Unless it is with my help,	
	For that is our arrangement.	
	I am the head of all the servants	
	My master keeps.	
	For the business that you offer me	
	I ask the price of a penny drink in my hand,	
	And then you can talk to her, noble warrior,	
	As much as your heart desires.	
REINHOUT:	A penny is easily spent,	
	That won't buy you much!	700
	Run, hurry, as fast as you can	
	And let me speak to Sanderijn—	
	Here are two pennies of pure gold—	
	And tell her with sincere words	
	That there is a messenger from Denmark	
	Who must speak to her urgently.	
THE KNIGHT'S FORESTER:	Now I'll run quickly	
	And return with the lady.	

[*Exit* THE KNIGHT'S FORESTER *to return with* SANDERIJN]

	O noble woman, of a free heart,	
	I pray you, please come with me.	710
	Here outside, a noble knight	
	Urgently wants to talk to you.	
REINHOUT	[*coming forward*]: O noble woman, loyal and good,	
	God who made all things,	
	Give you good day,	
	Beautiful maid, Sanderijn,	
SANDERIJN:	Reinhout, you are welcome.	
	Now tell me, what brings you here?	

REINHOUT:	I will tell you, worthy woman:	
	You must come with me,	720
	For Lanseloet, the free knight,	
	Has been looking for you everywhere.	
	His last words were his command to me,	
	Which was, if I could find you,	
	Noble lady, that I should bring you to him.	
	He wants to make you his bride.	
SANDERIJN:	Reinhout, my friend, that game is finished,	
	Tell him to find another one.	
	I care less about Lanseloet's love than	
	I care about a blade of grass.	730
REINHOUT:	O beautiful maid, you should see the state	
	He's in and his great misfortune.	
	Ever since he first lost you,	
	Noble lady, he has mourned,	
	He suffers torment,	
	And he lives in anguish.	
	It will surely kill him	
	If he cannot win you,	
	For I know that he loves you truly	
	Above anyone on earth.	740
	He has sworn on his knighthood,	
	If he could find your whereabouts,	
	Even if his family would suffer,	
	He would make you his wife.	
SANDERIJN:	Reinhout, things must stay as they are,	
	For here I am truly well loved.	
	I have married a nobleman	
	Whom I love above life itself	
	And I do not want to leave him.	
	Even if Lanseloet were as rich	750
	As Hector of Troy,	
	Even if God had allowed him	
	To wear the same crown	
	Alexander wore,	

| | I still would not choose him.
| | I would rather have my husband
| | Who gives me all his respect.
| | To him I will always be blissfully loyal.
| REINHOUT: | O Sanderijn, truly beautiful woman,
| | If he cannot have you, 760
| | Then he must forever live in sorrow,
| | Pining and tormented;
| | And you'll always regret
| | That you have gotten married,
| | Because the noble lord, Lanseloet,
| | Would have married you himself.
| SANDERIJN: | That's one thing I will not regret,
| | One thing I'll never be sorry about,
| | For I have never seen a man on earth
| | Whom I honor more 770
| | Than my dear husband.
| | It is right because he truly deserves it.
| | He is a knight with a great reputation.
| | He is a valiant knight, of proud demeanor,
| | Well-born and rich in wealth.
| | He is prudent and he is wise.
| | He is good with weapons,
| | And he has done great deeds.
| | My heart loves him faithfully and
| | Above all creatures. 780
| | Now I don't want to talk further.
| | Reinhout, go with haste,
| | And tell Lanseloet, your lord,
| | That he never should think of me again.
| REINHOUT: | O noble lady, of a free heart,
| | Since it has to be this way,
| | I pray you, good and noble lady,
| | To give me a sign, that I,
| | With certainty, can prove that I have seen you
| | And spoken with you. 790

SANDERIJN: Reinhout, that you shall have.
I will give you proof
That is both proper and excellent.
You will tell the free knight
That we stood, he and I,
In a beautiful green orchard,
And that there came a high-born
And noble falcon of the highest degree,
Who landed on a branch
Which was full of blossoms — 800
This you will tell the knight exactly —
And that the falcon who came there
Took a bloom from the branch
And left all the other blossoms alone.
He began to beat his wings
And he flew away in great haste;
This you will tell your noble friend.
Soon thereafter, the falcon came again
And he sought the branch up and down,
But he could not find her.[11] 810
And because he could not find the branch
The falcon suffered greatly;
This you will say to the noble warrior.
When you unfold my tale to him
He will surely believe
That you have seen and spoken to me,
Now I have finished what I have to say.
Reinhout, God preserve you!
     [*Exit* SANDERIJN]

REINHOUT: O Lord God, now I must go
And leave the beautiful lady behind! 820
I don't know what I should do,
How shall I deliver this message?
Tell him the whole truth,
That she is alive and that she is loved?

I know this will cause us all sorrow.
He will want that beautiful maid.
And I know truly it will cost him his life,
And the lives of all those who help him;
He will bring into danger
All of his kinsmen.[12] 830
Of these most will suffer
A bitter death, that I already know and
His trouble would be for naught
Because he cannot win her.
He will bring himself to despair
And bring with him also the great lords.
I shall change my story
And I will say that she is dead.

[REINHOUT *arriving in Denmark*]

Where are you, high-born comrade
Of Denmark, knight unmatched? 840

LANSELOET: Welcome to you, dear friend Reinhout.
A hearty welcome to you.
Have you found out anything
About Sanderijn? Tell me!

REINHOUT: O noble lord of a free heart,
I have sought her in many lands.
Finally I found the beauty
In a country called Rawast,
A place which lies in Africa,[13]
That's where this excellent lady traveled to, 850
And there, Lanseloet, free and noble prince,
I found the beautiful lady.
But talk of you
Cost her noble life;
When she heard about you
Her dear heart broke.

LANSELOET: Reinhout, these are all lies!
I can hear that you are lying to me.

	I don't want you to deceive me,	
	Tell me the truth!	860
	Show me a sign from her	
	Before I believe you.	
REINHOUT:	Lanseloet, high-born man,	
	I will give it to you exactly,	
	In a sign, proper and excellent,	
	That the pure lady gave to me.	
	She told me, that you two	
	Stood in a beautiful green orchard,	
	And that there came a falcon of high birth,	
	A noble falcon of great worth,	870
	Who landed on a branch	
	Which was full of blossoms.	
	This is what she asked me to tell you, lord,	
	goodly knight,	
	And that the falcon who came there,	
	Took a blossom from the branch, And left all the other blossoms alone.	
	He began to beat his wings,	
	And he flew away in great haste.	
	That's what she told me, high born friend.	
	And thereafter, the falcon came again,	880
	And he sought the branch up and down,	
	But he could not find her.	
	And then, because he could not find the branch,	
	The falcon suffered greatly.	
	This sign, noble warrior,	
	Is what the free lady gave me,	
	And then she turned her countenance from me	
	And spoke never again another word.	
LANSELOET:	O heavenly king, great lord,	
	That's a sign proper and excellent,	890
	And I do believe in it.	
	But tell me Reinhout, is she dead?	
REINHOUT:	Yes she is, high-born friend,	

And buried in the ground.
Here Lanseloet laments and then dies[14]

LANSELOET: O Sanderijn, you were the branch
That blossomed so beautifully,
And I was the falcon,
Who took a bloom away, this I know.
Now because I lost that noble bough, 900
I will never have peace again.
I will be tormented ever more
For the love of my lady.
All the joy I possessed on earth
Has turned to pain!
Mirror to all women
I have seen on earth!
Rightly I call, "O Lord have mercy"
For the mother who bore me,
Gave me counsel so cruel 910
That it made her heart leap with joy.
Alas, the bitter day
And the tragic shame
That she asked me to speak the words
With which I lost that beautiful lady.
It cost her life and it shall cost me mine as well
For my heart has been cut in two.
I wish it would split
So I could end my life,
For whatever I turn to 920
I am forever joyless.
She, whom I chose with a good heart,
With cruel counsel I have lost.
My heart lives in torment.
I shall die of grief.
I hope to see her in heaven,
And in that hope I die.
O, merciful God of heaven's kingdom,

	Now receive her soul and mine,	
	For I am finished with life.	930
	[LANSELOET *dies*]	
REINHOUT	[*coming forward*]: Lords and Ladies,	
	wives and husbands,	
	Please take this as an example.	
	For if you would love truly,	
	If you want to win your beloved,	
	Speak your love to her with courteous words.	
	Because this noble man of Denmark	
	Listened to a cruel counsel and by speaking	
	badly	
	Sustained the injury	
	That cost him his noble life.	
	Even though he loved the	940
	Beautiful lady above his life,	
	By the false advice that was given him	
	He spoke cruel words	
	And extinguished his true love	
	And forced her to steal away from him.	
	Therefore I advise above all things	
	That every man speak courteously,	
	Whenever he can or might;	
	And especially to all women	
	Speak courteously and truly	950
	So you will keep a woman's trust.	
	Now I pray you all who have been silent;	
	Our play is done,[15]	
	They will now play for you a farce.	

NOTES

[1] In the text, mother, "moeder," is written "moerder," murderer. Most editors correct the word as an error. Van Kammen points out that given the role of Lanseloet's mother in the play, the scribe may have made this "error" expressly, or not corrected it because of the dual role,

mother/murderer, in the play (163).

2 This line meaning: Mary is a woman firstly, above all things first; Mary is a woman above all other women; Mary is a woman above, over, all mankind.

3 In other words, it doesn't take much to convince most people, it just takes a little bit of faith in the proposition.

4 The feminine gender of "Love," "minne" and its pronouns in Middle Dutch, I translate as feminine in English.

5 A rich and complex line, "Op dat ic metter maget mach hoven," the last two words: to make a feast, to eat, with the vulgar implication, to fool around; also, get together, set up house, to belong to a court together. Verdam, 260.

6 Original rubric.

7 At this point Sanderijn is already far from Denmark. We will later learn from "The Knight's Forester" (590–605) that this fountain is situated in the land of the future husband of Sanderijn, which, according to Reinhout (847–9) is in Africa . . . though this may be a ruse to keep Lanseloet from discovering that Sanderijn is still alive.

8 Original rubric, repeated subsequently.

9 See note to v. 234.

10 Here the events have taken place a year ago in contradiction to the Knight's Forester's assertion at v. 594 that his lord met Sanderijn yesterday.

11 Both "branch," "gheerde" and its pronouns, "haren," her (genitive), and "si/se," her (accusative) reveal the distinctly feminine nature of the violated branch in Sanderijn's tale. The same will be true when Reinhout retells the tale to Lanseloet at the end of the play, v. 863–88.

12 In other words, he will risk his entire clan for her sake.

13 "Rawast" might be "Rabat," in Morocco, which, according to Roemans and van Assche (139), is also mentioned in *Tvoyage van Mher Joos van Ghistele* (1481–85), suggesting a real and not imaginary place in Africa, where Sanderijn now lives.

14 Original rubric.

15 "Voerspel," is really the first play or the first part of the performance, see the conclusion of *Esmoreit* for a similar direction.

P. Bruegel, "Two Peasant Women." Berlin-Dahlem, Staatliche Museen.

The Witch
"Die Hexe"

Dramatis Personae

Three women:
    MACHTELT, the Duke of Bruuyswijc
    LUUTGAERT, his uncle
    JULIANE, a counselor

Here begins the farce

MACHTELT: O good people, what shall I do?
    Wool is better than thread,
    But with me everything runs in reverse.
    Why is it all going so badly?
    I don't know what's happening to me!
    It must be the devil—
    Why else do I feel so crazed?
LUUTGAERT: Now tell me, truly,
    Why are you complaining like this?
    I have just chased off the fox   10
    Who killed two of my chickens.
    Why are you sitting here like this?
    Tell me now, what's happened?
MACHTELT: Luutgaert, I have good reason.
    It's a miracle I'm not crazy.
    Fate has laid me so low[1]
    That although I try my best, night and day,
    I cannot get ahead an inch.
    It must be witchcraft!
LUUTGAERT: Machtelt, by the Virgin Mary,   20
    I know you are not making this up.

            I too have been done in by magic
            And it might be the same for you!
            My cow has lost all her milk,
            It's nothing but water!
            It must be the fault of that tomcat from hell,[2]
            Or perhaps the cruel Satan,
            It couldn't be like this otherwise.
            Still . . . I have my suspicions about someone. . . .
            Yesterday when I was walking all alone   30
            I came upon the crossing of two roads; at the side
            I saw an old hag sitting[3]
            With a pot of butter she was selling.
            I'm sure she called on the devil
            To conjure that butter for her.
MACHTELT: Luutgaert, by God's almighty power,
            I'll tell it to you straight,
            She stole that butter from me.
            We should murder her and with a dull knife too!
            This whole month I have not gotten   40
            A pat of butter from my dappled cow.
            No matter how hard I whip or beat it,
            It always turns to slop.
            Are you sure you know her?
            Does that stinking whore live nearby?
LUUTGAERT: You bet she does, believe me:
            She was born in Kortrijk
            And there she lost an ear
            Because of her dirty tricks.
            And then she was banned from Gent,   50
            Her sentence was to be buried alive!
            She's mixed up with many things
            That are foul.
            Don't you know her? It's Juliane,
            Who lives up there on the corner.
            Now she sells German beer.
            She has a magic book

The Witch

	With which she casts spells.	
	It's too bad she's not lying	
	In a pit under the gallows,	60
	Her belly covered deep in earth.	
MACHTELT:	Luutgaert, what are we sitting here for then?	
	I know her well, this Juliane.	
	Let us both decide to go	
	And drink a pot of beer.	
	We will know the whole truth	
	Of this matter, every little bit.	
LUUTGAERT:	Gladly, Machtelt, may a great misfortune	
	Come her way from Saint Brigitta,	
	For I have suffered bad luck	70
	Too often because of her.	

[*They go to find* JULIANE *at her tavern*]

MACHTELT:	Tell us, lady Juliane,	
	Have you any German beer?	
JULIANE:	Of course, ladies. But, tell me ladies, how is it	
	That you ended up all the way out here?	
	You must have a reason,	
	Tell me, and you can count on my help.	
LUUTGAERT:	Juliane, we do have something we want to know.	
	But first we'd like to have some of your beer.	
	I bid you, find us a seat by the fire,	80
	Bring us our beer and we will pay you.	
JULIANE:	I'll ask no more and fetch your beer.	
	Just let me know what I can get you.	

[JULIANE *fetches the beer and returns*]

MACHTELT:	Dame Juliane, there's something that's
	bothering us,
	And we'd really like to ask you about it
	But we just don't dare.
	We know that you are wise.
	If we could, we would really like to
	Come into property.

	We have been given to believe that you could	90
	help us,	
	If you wanted to,	
	And that's why we've come to you.	
JULIANE:	Well, neighbor girls, if I can help you	
	With my advice and my experience	
	I will gladly do so.	
	[*in a conspiratorial way*] If things went well for you	
	it would make me happy too.	
	If you had the hand of a thief,	
	For which nine masses had been read,	
	Then you would always have good luck	
	in any dealings	
	To which you lent this hand.[4]	100
LUUTGAERT:	You whore, what you just said	
	Will cost you years of misery.	
	Now it is completely clear	
	What you've done to us.	
	You will have to repay us	
	Because you have stolen from us most cruelly,	
	Or we will pull your eyes out,	
	And will hit you so hard with this beer pot	
	That your brains will bug out of your head.	
	Here they fight[5]	110
JULIANE:	O ladies, hit me more softly!	

Notes

1. "Avonture," or "aventure," is fate, as well as strange or wonderful occurences, chance and luck.
2. "Helsche cater," literally, the tomcat from hell, generally another name for the devil.
3. "Teve," or hag also has the implication of "bitch," referring to, as it does in English, females of the canine as well as the human species.
4. The hand of a thief was supposed to provide power and good fortune to the bearer of that hand but only if he (or she) were another thief. Juliane's insult here is that to get rich her neighbors would have to turn to robbery (or that perhaps they already are thieves).
5. Original rubric.

P. Bruegel, "Summer." Hamburg, Kunsthalle.

Of the Winter and of the Summer

An abel spel about the Winter and the Summer,
and the farce which follows it.

Dramatis Personae

The SUMMER
The WINTER
LOIAERT
MOIAERT
CLAPPAERT
BOLLAERT
The COCKIJN
VENUS

PROLOGUE

  Ladies and gentlemen, husbands and wives,
  I ask God in whose power it lies
  To give us his grace
  So that we may live forever,
  For this I ask him, God be willing.
  Now you shall see and come to know,
  Ladies and gentlemen gathered here,
  How Winter and Summer strove,
  And you shall hear both sides.
  Now be still and make no noise,   10
  Watch and mark how it begins.
  I ask you to pay close attention

To the words of the debate between
Summer and Winter
Because this play is noble and true.
Summer is on his way,
You can be sure he will come.
Now calm down and stop your racket,
This I kindly ask you who are gathered.
I commend you to God, our heavenly father.   20

    [Enter WINTER and SUMMER]

SUMMER: I am the Summer and I make
The birds in the sky sing, the flowers bloom,
The leaves of the forest bud,
Ending the cold of Winter.
I usher in the sweet time
When the new flowers sprout—
Those which Winter has hidden.
I make many a man happy
Because he can go and play with his sweetheart;
So I bring many a man sweet mornings   30
With dew all through the day
When he can go out with his beloved
To play in the valley of love;
O, that is a joy above all,
To pick those flowers covered with dew.

WINTER: Fool, do hold your tongue!
I am the Winter, who controls everyone.
The birds who sing in Summer,
I can silence just like that.
When I work my art   40
And pull the violent wind from the east
I can make everything follow my will.
I'll make many a man's teeth chatter and
I'll make them beat their sides
So hard their fingers will split.[1]
Because of the icy cold

I can make pigs cry in the street.
You should leave off your bragging
Because I have everything in my power.
I control all the animals,
I can end the little bird's song and
I can make the fish in the rivers
Live under ice.

SUMMER: Lord Winter, I know your ways;
You are cruel in nature
And mean.
Many who live happily in Summer,
Dread you in their hearts.
When I come according to my ways,
They forget all the suffering
They have borne in Winter.
I let every man live in peace,
All those whom you kept indoors.
When the flowers bud,
Mankind knows it is Summer again.
I am loved by many, especially
By those who hate you because you are so cruel.

WINTER: Lord Summer, all this I know quite well,
There are some who do not long for me.
These are the ones who have spent
All their money in the tavern,
Drinking and gambling so happily
That they no longer can buy clothes.
In Summer they lie in the sun,
Thinking that it will always shine.
Then when I come with my storms
Bringing hail and cold snow
I cause these ones such grief
That their arms shake from cold.
These are the ones who live a lazy life,
The ones who depend too much on you.
I make them shiver in the streets,

	Even if they are young noblemen.	
	In this way I can check those	
	Who have not saved their money.	
SUMMER:	Lord Winter, you have a cruel nature—	
	This is easy to see.	
	But I am truly surprised	
	That you have set yourself against me,	
	For all the world is on my side	90
	Because I am so naturally noble.	
	I am the one who fills their cellars,	
	And who makes all the fruits grow.	
	I bring in the soft air,	
	The sweet Summer is my doing.	
	I make every orchard blossom	
	Which Winter's left fruitless.	
WINTER:	That's why I have to be superior,	
	Because I control all things.	
	You cannot prove otherwise, for	100
	I am the lord and you are my servant.	
LOIAERT:[2]	By God, Lord Winter, you are right,	
	What Summer makes grow,	
	Winter consumes.	
	When it is cold in the street,	
	When no one can bear the cold any longer,	
	Then we all sit 'round the fire,	
	Eating and drinking good beer,	
	Having bread, wine, meat and fish,	
	All brought to our table	110
	As we sit stuffed by the fire.	
	All that Summer can do	
	Winter consumes entirely.	
	If we were to tell the truth,	
	The sun is merely a slave.	
	Besides, the hot days are unending,	
	I grow sick of work	
	During those long days.	

Of the Winter and of the Summer

	I take the Winter for my lord.	
MOIAERT:[3]	Lord Loiaert, you are really out of line,	120
	To be so cruel to Summer,	
	Who often brings us	
	So much joy, merriment and play.	
	In Summer many mouths kiss	
	Secretly, behind green bushes.	
	Then people do what in Winter cannot be done.	
	When the flowers bloom in the valleys	
	And the birds make their song,	
	Each to his own kind,	
	Then there is no creature on earth	130
	Whose heart is not glad.	
	Ladies and gentlemen, husbands and wives,	
	All hearts grow bigger with joy	
	When the sweet Summertime comes,	
	With its beautiful flowers, with its sweet herbs.	
	When the birds begin to sing,	
	Then we can play the game of love	
	In secret places where the flowers smell	
	so sweet —	
	Those flowers which in Winter we must	
	go without,	
	For Winter is too cruel.	140
	This I know well.	
CLAPPAERT:[4]	Now here I am, I'm called Clappaert,	
	And I will tell you the whole truth.	
	I swear by God, the heavenly father,	
	That my lord, the Winter, also does a good job	
	Of playing — that I'm sure of —	
	The game of love, the one you talk of.	
	When two lovers lie on top	
	Of the bed all naked as can be,	
	Then and there much joy will be made	150
	Even if there are no birds singing.	
	The nights are cold and long too, but	

| | The cold makes us crawl to each other,
| | Each between the other's legs.
| | To this my Lord Winter compels us all,
| | And in this manner brings us together,
| | That everyone plays the game of love.
| | I say all this and it is no lie
| | For I truly know it's right.
| | In Summer the nights are really too hot. 160
| | One lies here and the other there.
| | They dare not come closer to each other,
| | That's what the heat of the season does,
| | But in the Winter they press together,
| | side by side,
| | Their pudenda glued fast together.
| WINTER: | By God, Clappaert, you are right
| | And you have spoken well.
| | I wouldn't like to disrupt the game of love
| | In any way.
| | I'd rather give everyone a red mouth 170
| | From kissing all those long nights.
| | All in a little bed, sweet and soft,
| | Lie sleeping two lovers
| | And there they give pleasure to each other.
| | Love's game is played in Winter as well,
| | Even if it isn't in an orchard
| | Where the birds may sing.
| BOLLAERT:[5] | Lord Winter, you would like to triumph over
| | The Summer, but it shall not be.
| | I would rather give up my life 180
| | Than let that happen,
| | For you bring nothing but cold,
| | Rain, hail, and icy snow.
| | You make everyone so unhappy
| | That they forget all their joy,
| | While my lord the Summer
| | Fills the wretch with joy

	Who lies in the ashes	
	By the fire.	
	Winter, I can find no manners in you;	190
	Therefore you must be the lesser lord of two.	
WINTER:	Lord Bollaert, it really surprises me	
	To hear you talk like this.	
	You really can't sustain your point,	
	For I must be the greater one.	
	I take away the Summer's hot sun,	
	And I keep back the clear sky,	
	And I consume all the fruits	
	That Summer has been able to get.	
	On the earth there's neither man nor woman	200
	Who can avoid serving me.	
	I challenge you to the debate,	
	To see whether I shall remain the superior.	
MOIAERT:	Now I can no longer keep silent	
	While the truth is being ignored.	
	Lord Winter, you would die of hunger	
	Without the Summer, that high lord.	
	My dear Winter, what would you do	
	If the Summer did not lend you his grace,	
	He, who makes things grow, both now and	210
	in the time to come?	
	The bread and wine by which you live,	
	where would you find it?	
	All that man has in the world,	
	Through Summer's power is made to flower,	
	Apples, pears, and other fruit,	
	Those which the whole world lives on.	
	If you were clever or wise,	
	You would bow down before him.	
CLAPPAERT:	Lord Moiaert, be silent,	
	Winter is much too strong for you.	
	When I take a good look at you,	220
	I see that your lips are blue with cold.	

SUMMER:	By God, I see you're not feeling very warm, yourself,
	You're not exactly basking in the heat!
	I see that the cold has taken its toll on you too,
	Even if you did argue so proudly.
	By God, Lord Winter, this will be avenged,
	This high and mighty talk.
	When the blossoms in the valleys
	Sway, smelling and blooming so sweetly,
	And the sun in his throne 230
	Shines so pleasantly and warmly,
	Then man on earth will find nothing
	That will not flower or bear fruit,
	Then fear for your life, Lord Winter,
	For you might lose your power.
BOLLAERT:	And then you'll feel the sweet nights coming on,
	With noble dew in the valleys,
	And then the nightingale will sing,
	And the flowers will sprout through the green,
	White and red, each according to its own way, 240
	And then the trees will be filled with blossoms
	And in each heart happiness will grow,
	And then love will double the happiness.
WINTER:	Now I have never heard anything so amazing.
	You speak the truth — it amazes me —
	If I were to banish love
	Then certainly it would not come in Winter.
	But on this point I want to be clear,
	That people also love in the Winter,
	And often they love more 250
	Than in the Summer, rest assured,
	Even if the dew is not sweet,
	The nights are long, do you know what I mean?
	Everyone has a story.
	Two lovers, there they are,
	Both with their little loves
	Throwing their arms about each other

To keep each other warm.
Naturally, the cold drives them to this.
Even if the nightingale isn't singing,
Love's game is always played. . . .
More than in Summer, of that I am sure!
I'll bet my life on it!

SUMMER: At the risk of being bold
I will contest you.
The happier the season the happier the heart,
The happier the heart the more the love-making.
When the Summer comes to men,
And the flowers burst forth and blossom,
And the little birds sing a melody,
Then all hearts will be proud,
Because the Summer is so gracious
And so noble in nature.
Even if a heart is angry and sour,
When the Summer comes to the earth
It will be filled with joy
Because the Winter has been put down.
The tongues of man and bird
Are silent in winter
Because everyone must stay inside
When it has snowed and everything is
                        frozen over.
In Winter, man's life is truly made mean
Because of the suffering he endures.
But in Summer, he is happy
Because it is the time when he sees the
                        shining sun again.
Lord Winter, with this argument you must
Be won, if you would only acknowledge
                        the truth.

WINTER: In that case you should begin in another key,
That is, if you'd like to beat me.
My supporters are many,

>   Why should I give up?
>   Why should I lose this match?
>   To give up is to be cursed by God!
>   Out of respect for Venus, who wears a crown,
>   The Queen of love,
>   Whom you claim is yours,
>   I say that I have all in my power
>   That live under heaven's throne.
>   That people practice love most in Summer
>   And that in Winter they come up short,   300
>   This I do contest,
>   On this point you are a liar,
>   Bet your life against mine —
>   Shorten it to fit between two sunrises —
>   That love happens more often
>   In Winter — which it surely does —
>   Than in Summer — that's what you think —
>   Well, in this debate I want to win first prize
>   in the name of
>   Venus, the Queen of love,
>   And thereby do her honor.   310
>   Throw down your gauntlet, if you're up to it.
> SUMMER: Now, I have never been so happy
>   As I am this minute,
>   Knowing that I shall make so many creatures
>   Happy and full of joy.
>   It has fallen to me
>   To contest you.
>   I shall cause you such shame,
>   That I shall outlast you in the fight,
>   And thus I will drive you away   320
>   And it will be Summer always.
> COCKIJN:[6] For this my heart is glad.
>   Lord Summer, you will give him his due.
>   Lord Winter, you have been so cruel to me
>   That I have not dared to speak.

I know your tricks well.
You have given me so much poverty
That now I prize the Summer's prosperity,
For he makes my heart joyful
Like all the other tramps 330
Who lie in the ashes to keep warm.
We are joyful
When the Summer comes, mercifully,
To drive you away from here.
You forced me to sit by the fire
In the ashes just like the chickens.
That's why I love the Summer and
Why he will rout you!
You have done me many bad turns,
Making me sit in the ashes by the fire. 340
Lord Winter, you have been here much too long
For my taste, get out of here!
You have forced me to sit in the stench,
And in the smoke, to my detriment.
That's why I love the Summer,
He, the one who will kill you.

WINTER: Get you hence, you foul caitiff,
With your big talk.
I will bring you to such shame
That you will regret it all your life. 350
I will make you shiver with cold;
I'll burn the marrow out of your shins.
Foul caitiff, get out of here.
Lord Summer, I publicly say to you,
You must put up a guarantee,
That I may enter without worry
Into a contest with you, Lord Summer.

[*Exit or retire upstage*, SUMMER *and* WINTER]

COCKIJN: God damn it,
I'll put up the guarantee!

	I love the noble Summer	360
	With all my heart,	
	The excellent Summer, that courageous warrior.	
	I'll put up as bond all my land	
	And my life and all my goods,	
	So he can come proudly	
	To challenge you in the debate, Lord Winter.	
CLAPPAERT:	Be quiet right now, you mean thing,	
	In the devil's name, get out of here,	
	And go sit by the fire,	
	Because you're so terribly cold!	370
	You go about wearing nothing but rags.	
	You're really a perfect tramp,	
	You must have come from the flea market,	
	Because it looks like you've sold everything you have!	
	Which devil brought you here?	
	You look like a real layabout to me.	
	I can see from your looks	
	That Summer would be the perfect cure for you!	
	I know that if you had money	
	You'd gamble away with all your might.	380
	Friend, you are not needed here,	
	Stand aside!	
COCKIJN:	Look boy, if I were wearing fancy clothes,	
	Then I'd get some respect;	
	But now I'm gettin' chewed out for dressing like a tramp —	
	Just because I'm not well-dressed.	
	All this time I have lived my life	
	With rogues among the tramps.	
	A flea stands more readily at my disposal	
	Than a cloak of scarlet red.	390
	But if the cruel Winter were dead,	
	Then my heart would live in peace.	
	God must give the Summer victory,	

OF THE WINTER AND OF THE SUMMER 207

	He should win the fight.	
MOIAERT:	Lord Winter, following the rules of the debate,
	I will be the second of that high nobleman, Summer,
	He who will come as a lion
	To protect his honor in this contest.
	Lord Winter, because you are the challenger,
	You too must follow the rules of the duel.	400
CLAPPAERT:	Now I want people to value Winter so
	I will be his second instantly,
	So that he will come as a courageous hero,
	Able to make good his challenge.
	God give him good luck,
	So he will remain in his honored place.
	Now go to him with all speed,
	While Winter will prepare himself.
	[*Exit all, except* MOIAERT]
MOIAERT:	Oh God, who will judge the match,
	This quarrel, between these two lords?	410
	All the world will be lost.
	If the Summer is vanquished . . .
	Or if Winter will be killed off,
	A quarter of the year will be lost in this duel.
	It will be a disaster
	No matter which side is vanquished.
	Truly I don't know
	How to stop all this,
	For they are both quite resolved
	And today they have both solemnly sworn.	420
	There is on earth no one born
	Who could, with all his might, prevent this. . . .
	Wait a minute, I've got it!
	I will go with a humble heart
	To the goddess, Venus,
	Who is a woman above all.
	I hope that she will be able to break this match,

I will go to her, that noble and good woman,
                              Venus,
And tell her
How the matter lies.   430
I'm sure she will not leave it like this,
She will take this battle upon herself.
Now I will run like a young page
To my lady Venus.
If we lose Summer and with it, the sunshine,
Then for most of us happiness will be lost also.

> [*Calling her*]

Where are you, high-born lady,
Venus, noble Queen?

> [*Enter* VENUS]

VENUS: Tell me, friend, in sweet phrases,
On what business are you here?   440
MOIAERT: Lady, I'll tell it to you openly.
It's about two-high born lords,
Who have bound each other to the death —
They have challenged each other to a duel.
Before vespers tomorrow
They have sworn to see each other dead.
There is no one on earth so powerful
Who can take up this cause,
Nether lord nor lady, wife nor husband,
No one but you, lady, alone.   450
These two lords are not insignificant.
The one is the Summer, rich in possessions,
The other, the Winter, who equals him there —
They have gotten into a tiff
And it has all come to a head
Because of you, O noble lady.
Never will this be decided,
If you will not help.
VENUS: Dear friend, tell me,

OF THE WINTER AND OF THE SUMMER

                How did it come to this?
                You say it happened because of me,
                And yet, I'm completely blameless.
MOIAERT: Lady, I want you to understand.
                They have argued with sharp words.
                There were many who heard them,
                They accused each other,
                And each boasted
                His own deeds, his own powers.
                Then the Summer spoke out before all
                That he was beautiful and gracious
                And that he filled all good hearts
                With bliss and joy.
                He claimed that people more often
                Find love in the Summer time
                Than in Winter, noble lady,
                That was what he said, you know.
                Then the cruel Winter stepped forth,
                And he became angry and cross.
                And then he took a glove
                And with it dared the Summer to a duel;
                Then the Summer, with a quick shot,
                Took up his glove,
                So accepting his challenge.
                They took seconds on each side.
                Noble lady, take up this strife,
                Because you have the power to help.
                The Winter is the fiercer foe, and
                I fear for my Lord, the Summer.
VENUS: Friend, I will be quick.
                I'll be there tomorrow,
                Before the sun has risen.
                I will be there in good time.
                Before these lords enter into the duel,
                I will come to take up both sides
                Because if I let these two lords fight,

	Then we would see many extraordinary	
	things happen!	
	If either of the two is vanquished	
	Then the world will be lost.	
	I shall take up this dispute,	
	Because the power is mine to yield.	500
MOIAERT:	O noble lady, then I will	
	Return with a happy heart.	
	You will surely bring all to good,	
	That I know for certain.	
	There is no one on earth	
	Who can end this as well as you.	
VENUS:	Friend, I shall be there,	
	Before the sun is up tomorrow.	

[*Exit* VENUS]

MOIAERT:	This looks like the best way to me.	
	It's better that the contest be disbanded	510
	Because if either of the two is killed	
	It would be the source of great suffering.	
	If my Lord the Summer should die,	
	Then we'd all be in for a rough time,	
	For the Winter will spare us nothing —	
	He is so bad and cruel at heart.	

[*Exit* MOIAERT]

[*The next day, enter* WINTER *and* SUMMER, *respectively*]

WINTER:	Now I am on my way	
	To the duel, as it suits me.	
	Here I call forth the Summer,	
	That he should come and defend his honor.	520
SUMMER:	Lord Winter, no more of your dares.	
	Think on this, I'm coming your way.	
	And the reason I've taken your challenge	
	Is so I can take your life.	
COCKIJN:	God, Lord above all,	

	Give the victory to Lord Summer,	
	Let him take Winter's life;	
	Then you will make me completely happy.	
	For Winter has often caused me great pain,	
	He makes my liver shiver with cold!	530
	[*Enter* VENUS]	
VENUS:	My lords, I bid you, give over to me	
	This debate and this strife,	
	For you two are brothers.	
	To me, his behavior seems ill-suited to	
	your standing,	
	This calling each other out to duel,	
	And this trying to kill each other!	
	Lord Summer, will you let me make the decision?	
	This I ask you whose true profession is love.	
SUMMER:	Lady Venus, noble queen,	
	I will do so, but not gladly.	540
	Because you are the Queen of Love	
	I don't want to deny you, and	
	Therefore I will give over this strife to you.	
	Do with it what you will.	
	There is no one else on earth	
	For whom I would do this bidding.	
VENUS:	Lord Summer I will	
	Thank you for this eternally.	
	Now I pray, Lord Winter,	
	That you will do the same for me.	550
WINTER:	Lady Venus, you wear the crown	
	And you are the Queen of Love.	
	Therefore I do not know how to begin	
	To refuse you what you ask.	
	Venus, my lady, you are worth a great deal to me,	
	I truly want to remain in your protection.	
VENUS:	Then from now on you shall never again fight,	
	And always you shall be brothers.	

            God made water and wine
            And all that men find on this earth.   560
            He made the firmament
            In which he put the seven planets,
            And there too the twelve signs of the zodiac,
            Who together have all in their power.
            They cause heat, they cause cold,
            They make it winter and summer,
            As the astronomers teach us.
            The one is cold, the other hot.
            Never can the time stand still,
            It must be either Winter or Summer,   570
            Sometimes the hot sunshine,
            Sometimes the hail and the cold snow.
            This shall be and shall never change.
            As long as the world exists,
            Each will work according to his nature,
            Because God has set it this way.
            If either of the two is disrupted,
            Summer or Winter equally,
            The time will stand still,
            Then everything that is on earth   580
            Will fade and perish.
            One without the other cannot be.

WINTER: Lady Venus, you have cured me,
            For your words are true.
            I must follow the Summer
            And the Summer must follow me.

SUMMER: This I know as well as you,
            That one without the other cannot be.
            But my sorrow and my complaint
            Is that you wanted to drive me out.   590
            When I spoke, you made me keep silent,
            You said that you were the boss.
            Lord Winter I know for certain that
            You are a tyrant

OF THE WINTER AND OF THE SUMMER

               To those whom I let live in joy
               When I come with my flowers.
VENUS: My lords, I have taken this up,
               To come between you two in this dispute;
               By your will and your consent,
               I have made clear my desire.   600
               Now let's not argue about it anymore.
               Instead, you shall forever be as brothers.
               Let us eat and drink wine
               And live in great happiness.
COCKIJN [*aside or alone*]: So now for the rest of my life
               I'll be under Winter's power.
               I couldn't begin to tell you
               How much suffering he's caused me.
               All this because Venus the Queen
               Came here — thanks for nothing!   610
               She came between them to take up the duel.
               The devil brought her here in time.
               I was already so glad
               Because Winter would have been vanquished.
               The Summer would have taken his life,
               He had such confidence . . .
               His weapons were so good
               And his sword was well made,
               Surely he would have killed him with it
               If they had come to duel.   620
               But Lady Venus had to take it up!
               I am sick at heart.
               I guess I'll go now, walking like a pig
               To Maastricht by the coals.[7]
               There I will hole up,
               Until the Summer comes again.

Notes

1. "Slaen met sinen handen," as in the Fries expression, "hanbukje" or "hanbuste," to warm one's hands by hitting one's sides. Stellinga, 41.
2. The lazy one.
3. The pretty one, the show-off, a pretty boy.
4. Loud-mouth, gossip.
5. Braggart, bag of wind, boaster.
6. Tramp, vagrant, free-loader.
7. A great deal has been written about this line and the one that follows it. It seems that Cockijn will go where he can wait out the Winter in the utmost comfort and where a brotherhood of tramps and vagrants might be found. Stellinga, 71.

P. Bruegel, "The Blue Cloak." *Netherlandish Proverbs.* Berlin-Dahlem, Staatliche Museen.

RUBBEN

Dramatis Personae

RUBBEN
Rubben's mother-in-law called, the WIFE
GOSEN, Rubben's father-in-law

Here begins the farce

RUBBEN: Oh boy, do I know,
I'm quite sure
That what's done in haste
Will later cause regret.
I myself have married a young wife.
It's been about three months since I married her
And yesterday evening when I came home
I found her delivered of a child.
Now I have often heard tell
That pregnancy lasts nine months. 10
But those who have seen the child
Say he wasn't born a minute too soon.
He's a big and good-looking kid,
All his limbs are well-developed,
His little nails and little toes all complete.
Could all this have happened in three months?
No one can tell me
That I fathered this child!
She must have started this
Long before I took her as my wife. 20
The devil be damned if I ever touched her
                                          before that!
Her mother never left me alone for a minute
                                          with her.

By God, she must have known her daughter's business
Better than I did, of that I'm sure.

[*Enter his mother-in-law*]

WIFE: Hey, Rubben, are you there?
Now tell me, how are things going with my daughter?

RUBBEN: In truth, woman, I don't know.
Your daughter has delivered a baby.
She's had a boy-child
Who looks to be about a half-year old. 30

WIFE: I thank God in every way
That she has survived the travail.

RUBBEN: I, for myself, am not happy that
She rushed things so much.
My heart is angry,
I do not know what to think or do.

WIFE: Why? What do you mean?
Tell me exactly what's troubling you.
I'm sure I can advise you
And help you feel more at peace. 40

RUBBEN: Really, if someone were trying to kill me,
I couldn't be more unhappy,
For today it is to the day
Three months since I took your daughter as my wife
And first came into her company,
Three months and five nights to be exact,
And now she has born a child,
Who looks about half a year old.
He's not missing a hair on his head
Nor a nail on his fingers or his toes. 50
Pregnancy lasts more or less
Nine months altogether.
I'll tell anyone who'll listen

	That I did not father that child.	
WIFE:	Christ, listen to this fellow!	
	On my word, you are completely crazy!	
RUBBEN:	I am not drunk,	
	I know exactly what I'm saying.	
	If I add one and two	
	That makes three, and then another five days.	60
WIFE:	Sweet lad, you've got it all wrong,	
	You haven't got the time right.	
	You know very well how you will be thought of	
	If you slander your wife like this.	
	Three months before and three months after	
	Plus three months in the middle	
	Makes all together nine,	
	This I know well.	
RUBBEN:	If you could convince me of this	
	Then you might as well call me Archimedes.[1]	70
	Still . . . I have some proof . . .	
	I had a cow that I sold at the time.	
	When a man wanted to buy it	
	He asked if he could do it on credit.	
	Yesterday evening he brought the money to me,	
	Three months was our agreement.	
	You may think I'm crazy,	
	But I did keep track of the time!	
WIFE:	Now I really can tell you're drunk,	
	Because three times three is nine.	80
	Here is my husband, our daughter's father,	
	I know he's sure of it too.	
	Hey, Gosen, are you ready?	
	Come here. I need to talk to you.	
GOSEN	[*entering*]: Christ, what's the problem?	
	Well, here I am, what'll it be?	
WIFE:	Now tell us, good Goswijn,[2]	
	Do you remember that our daughter wed?	
GOSEN:	Yes, truly she married a man.	

	It's been about three months now.	90
WIFE:	That was to the day today	
	Nine months ago, for those of us who can count,	
	But Rubben, our son, is really upset	
	That she has just been delivered of a child.	
	Even if it only took seven months,	
	Still it's all quite possible.	
GOSEN:	What, Rubben, son-in-law, I didn't see you.	
	Is our daughter delivered? May God preserve her!	
RUBBEN:	Yes, but I can't understand	
	How I could be its father.	100
	I venture to swear on my word of honor	
	That she has been mine for only three months.	
WIFE:	Plus the three months she was engaged,	
	Plus three months you're not counting,	
	And if you put all these together	
	It adds up to nine months.	
	That is just exactly the time	
	That a woman needs to bear a child.	
GOSEN:	It's true what she says,	
	In this she does not lie.	110
RUBBEN:	What, has the devil cuckolded me?	
	I, who know the truth so well by my cow.	
	But let me say more.	
	When I took your daughter to wife	
	And when I first went to bed with her	
	And I wanted to show her the way —	
	Woman, this I must tell you —	
	She knew it as well as I did.	
	She offered me her body	
	As if she'd been at it for at least seven years.	120
	I took this very hard.	
	I kept mum, but I was furious.	
GOSEN:	That's just what her mother did when I took her to wife,	
	When we first slept together.	

WIFE:	She also knew about all kinds of things As if I had had her for seven months. And how did that happen? I knew things from what I'd heard. For he who pays attention And remembers all that he hears tell, 130 Never has to have any experience. That's how it was with my daughter. Look dear fellow — and don't get all worked up — If you really want to know the truth The time at night slipped by you, You simply forgot to count the nights When you were happily enjoying My daughter, your young wife. When you were lying next to her beautiful body Happy and warm, 140 Each in the other's arms, You forgot the time. You counted the days When you saw the sun rising — but not the nights. Not a single woman can be pregnant Only during the day! This has always been the case, it's not a fib! You lost track of the time. If you want me to swear to the truth Then I will swear on the cross: 150 When my daughter came in your house She had no more experience, Nor any more longing for men, Than I did when I married her father.
GOSEN:	But by God, I was really furious then! Because you were so good at it, I thought, "This one's practiced somewhere With her friends." But you made me believe

	That you knew it all from the hearing	160
	and telling.	
RUBBEN:	Really, friend, women's ways	
	I've heard tell are hard to fathom.	
	But I would have rather had your daughter	
	As an apprentice than as a master....	
	What the devil, she was a pro,	
	She couldn't have amazed me more.	
WIFE:	That's because she thought it was your due,	
	And because she thought you really liked her.	
	Her heart was always happy	
	Whenever she saw you.	170
	The first words out of her mouth were always,	
	"If I have seen my dear Rubben,	
	Then the whole day will pass without trouble."	
	That was what she'd say.	
	It was this great love which ruled her,	
	Therefore she could not hide her feelings.	
	You don't have to puzzle about it any more.	
	My daughter was truly a virgin	
	[*aside*] Five years after she was born,	
	That I can swear on a pile of relics.	180
RUBBEN:	By God, it would always bother me,	
	If I had judged her wrongly.	
	But that the time had so slipped by me,	
	That's one thing I don't understand ...	
	I still have the feeling	
	That it's only been three months....	
WIFE:	Listen, dear boy, and be at peace.	
	I want to set the time right for you	
	And on these three fingers I will count.	
	The first three months I have here,	190
	The second three months she sat by the fire,	
	And the third three months were the nights,	
	Altogether the time is accounted for;	
	This adds up to nine months.	

	I swear to you by all the saints who have	
	children and fathers.	
	Don't worry about this ever again!	
GOSEN:	She tells the truth, by our Lord,	
	She can't have lied about this.	
RUBBEN:	Gosh, I would have been deceived by the devil!	
	If I forgot to count the nights,	200
	I'd have been upset for nothing.	
	If the fault is entirely mine	
	Then I would have always regretted	
	Disowning my wife.	
	Now I will go and quickly prepare her supper	
	To show her honor and respect,	
	And to thank God our dear Lord	
	That she has given me such a pretty child.	
WIFE:	Then do it, and make haste,	
	And put a pot of meat on the fire for us	210
	Because I am coming that way soon	
	To see how she's doing.	
RUBBEN:	That I will do with pleasure, God knows,	
	And I will make it delicious,	
	It will taste so good to you,	
	That you'll lick your fingers when you're done!	

[*Exit* RUBBEN]

WIFE:	That's how you have to fool men	
	When you're married to one,	
	Put him in a blue cloak	
	And pull a bag over his head.[3]	220
GOSEN:	You and your daughter are both whores!	
	You made Rubben swallow quite a tale.	
	I too have had those same thoughts	
	And later you have talked me out of them.	
WIFE:	I know, but let's not talk about it,	
	I don't want my good name to suffer.	
GOSEN:	You know so many sly tricks.	

| | If I see one thing, you'll convince me |
| | it's something else, |

If I see one thing, you'll convince me
                             it's something else,
Just as you did with Rubben.
You made him think three added up to nine,   230
You tricked him so well
That he can't think of a way around you.
But you and your kind know how to turn a trick,[4]
Leading many a man down the garden path,
Thinking he's married a virgin,
When, by God, her flower was picked long ago!
That's how it was when I married you, likewise
When our daughter took up with Rubben
She'd been playing hide the salami for a long time.

WIFE: Get down off the pulpit, will you!   240
Damn you to hell!
I'd like to smack you so hard on your snozzola
That your teeth would come popping out.

GOSEN: In that case, you first!

They fight[5]

Notes

1. In the original, the name is, "Hughe" a proper name which means intelligence. Comparing himself to "Hughe" (or as I translate it "Archimedes"), Rubben is saying, "I'd have to be really smart to figure it that way," i.e. your logic is corrupt and meant to deceive. Leendertz translates the name as a synonym for "crazy" (v. 2, 531), the line then meaning, "You might as well call me crazy"; according to Stellinga, there may be other implications here such as "gullible lout" or cuckold, Rubben, in *Vanden Winter* (Zutphen, 1966), 76.
2. Goeswijn is Gosen's last name, the name Goeswijn or Gosen is the equivalent of "God's friend." This same name appears in *De Buskenblazer* and it is traditionally a name for an unlucky, or stupid fellow in the later farces.
3. A version of cuckold and trick him: "ene blau hoyke an hanghen," to put on a blue cloak, is to deceive a spouse, to cuckold; the latter, "to pull a bag over his head," Stellinga suggests may refer to the prisoners who were gagged during punishment preventing them from talking. Stellinga, *Rubben*, 85.
4. "Your and yours," i.e., women.
5. Original rubric.

P. Bruegel, "A Maerte." National Museum, Stockholm.

Truwanten

Dramatis Personae

The WOMAN
The MAERTE, a serving girl or maid
The BROTHER
THE DEVIL

....
....

WOMAN:	Hurry up or I'll break your neck,
	You've let my animals go hungry.
	Have you been out fooling around?
	Come forward! Our Lady damn you!
MAERTE	[*entering*]: Be still, woman! Be satisfied
	With this bundle I carry.
	Never on any other day have I 110
	Gone so far to find food.
	You are right to be mad at me,
	But since I've been out my feet have not had
	a minute's rest.
WOMAN:	You whore! You should be burned!
	You rotten tripe sack.
MAERTE:	Lady, why are you cursing me
	Without my having earned it? I cannot bear it.
	I hope you get a cramp in your jaw!
	I won't let myself be slandered,
	Just give me my money, 120
	Working here has been bitter and hard.
WOMAN:	By Jesus! It's a bad year.
	Devil take all,
	I'll not keep you another minute.

	Hurry up! The devil can show you the way!	
MAERTE:	Lady, then I'll leave you.	
	[*alone*] God, who made everything, help me!	
	I've been done in . . .	
	To loose my job like this!	
	What Brother Everaet[1] told me	130
	Now seems to me proven true.	
	If I end up alone like he did	
	Then I must go through life as he does.	
	I'd better go to his school again . . .	
	In haste I'm off to the cloister.	

[*She leaves, going to* BROTHER EVERAET's *cell*]

	Do you hear me, Brother Everaet?	
	I am here, God bless me for it.	
BROTHER	[*coming out*]: O, my dear child, you are most welcome!	
	Now let me leave my hermit's cell.	
	I will lead you through the land,	140
	Pretending you are Sister Lute.	
	I know all sorts of tricks	
	That are unknown to anyone else.	
MAERTE:	What Brother Everaet, are you possessed?	
	Do you want to teach me to truant?[2]	
BROTHER:	Be quiet, dear child, by all the saints!	
	To be truant is not hard work.	
	Let's go, put on this mantle![3]	
	I would never give you bad advice,	
	For by the grace of dear God,	150
	In this land there is no morsel	
	That you and I will not share.	
	And many a good drop	
	Of wine shall pass through our lips too.	
	Now follow me, Sister Luutgaert!	
MAERTE:	Gladly, Brother Everaet.	

[*They journey along and we see them at their business begging*]

BROTHER	[*to his dupes*]:	

Help us God, we are so tired of walking,
From St. John the Lateran
To Jerusalem and the Holy Grave 160
We have wandered. Many more tough days
Must we still endure.
O, that you will enjoy everlasting life!
Will you give me and Sister Luten something
Of your goods, so that we can live.
Put something tasty in our trap
For it would please us very much,

[*To* SISTER LUUTGAERT *and the audience*]

All troubles we have left behind,
And we mean from now on to be truant.
Truancy works pretty well for us. 170
But still it's tough!
We have many colleagues,
Both hermits and in cloister cells,
Who barely see the light of the world.
If they'd just get to work, washing and weaving,[4]
They'd enter the kingdom of heaven
With bags full of goods.
But sisters, beguines, and lollards,
They are so very lazy
That they can hardly endure to be deprived, 180
They like to drink big drafts
If they get the chance.
With this I will end,
For I could say even more.
Good deeds are their own reward.

EPILOGUE

THE DEVIL [*alone or down stage*]: Listen gentlemen everywhere,
I have brought into the trap
This Brother through my craft.

His holiness is full of crap.
Even if he still wears a gray robe,   190
The right time will come
And he will make his reckoning,
He and his brothers, big and small,
Who truant about the land
And eat because of the sins and shames
                                    of the people.
One day they'll be singing all about it
When they're stewing in my kettle, that is!

Notes

1. "Broeder Everaet," a member of a loosely organized religious order of mendicants.
2. Like the title of the play, "truwanten," truant means to beg through choice rather than necessity, to be an idle rogue.
3. A pilgrim's mantle.
4. Washing, "vollen," is a stage in the production of cloth when the wool is de-fatted and cleaned.

Anon. (Dutch), "Overhand": *The Battle for the Breeches.*

Three Days Lord

Dramatis Personae

A MESSENGER
JAN
BETTE, his wife
Ghebuer, NEIGHBOR, also called Imberecht
Lijsbeth, his WIFE

A foolish farce,
A good farce.

MESSENGER: Now hear, you lords, and be still.
They say he doesn't have a lot of fun
Who's married to a shrewish wife.
His suffering is the worst,
For they say there's nothing
That will tame an angry wife.
And surely it is just, for we will show you,
Here, before your very eyes,
A good example of this matter.
Now be quiet and be still.   10
We will play it for you right away.

[*A tavern, enter* NEIGHBOR, *drunk, addressing the audience*]

NEIGHBOR:[1] We are going to play a piece of shit for you
That goes way above all your heads.
God give you shame and dishonor!
Go on home and mind your own business.
I know for sure that you have something at home,
That you'll discover early tomorrow morning.[2]
The bastard, he had to meddle with it!
And couldn't he have kept quiet?

We are playing here today because of him, 20
And all because of his stupid stories!
I'll go and sit at the bar,
And drink a hat full of beer by the fire.³
Tapster, tap some beer!
Tap it full, hurry yourself up!
God give him trouble who spares it today!
    [*Gets his beer*]
I will drink without sorrow,
I'll live now, die tomorrow.
Let's see, how'm I doing?
[*taking up his beer*] It smells fine, by St. John, 30
[*taking a sip*] And now I know how good it tastes.
See how these people all sit gaping!
Haven't you ever seen a man before?
               Do you want to buy me?
It seems to me that you don't have to go far
To catch a fool, you don't even need a net!
Ay, look at these gawking fools, by St. Nick's ass.⁴
I could catch more men than sparrows here.
I gotta have a drink now. [*takes another sip*]
Baa! What d'you think, 'going all right?
You're sitting here again for another play, 40
Well it's crazy for you to sit here.
    [*Enter* WIFE *and* JAN]

WIFE: What the devil, what have you done?
You've made a real mess of things.
I'm going to bonk you on your noggin!
Whatever you do, it's always wrong!⁵
    [*Exit* WIFE]

NEIGHBOR: Ay! I want you all to go
And get a pillow under your feet!
Maria, mother, sweet maid,
And true, you have no shame in you.

Three Days Lord

	Take a good look at me! Do you think	50
	I'm a scarecrow?	
	Something so strange no one has ever heard of.	
JAN:	Neighbor, you look pretty upset,	
	Is there something that's bothering you?	
NEIGHBOR:	Don't you see these folks who sit	
	And gape while I just sit here drinking?	
	It seems they never saw a man before.	
	[*noticing Jan's upset*] Dear neighbor,	
	get a hold of yourself, get a grip!	
JAN:	Neighbor, if that's all there is,	
	Neighbor, then I don't pity you very much,	
	For, by our dear Lord,	60
	Neighbor, you're complaining about nothing,	
	For if you had at home a wife	
	Like I have — I'll tell you frankly —	
	You'd quickly forget those people	
	About whom you are so angry.	
	Ah, neighbor, neighbor, neighbor,	
	If you knew how it is with those	
	Who have no clothes, no goods, no money,	
	And who always come home to find a shrew	
	for a wife!	
	They have suffering equal	70
	To those in the abyss of hell.	
NEIGHBOR:	Neighbor, now tell me as a friend,	
	What is it you're wanting, I long to know.	
JAN:	Neighbor, do you know what's wrong with me?	
	I have a shrewish wife, as you well know,	
	Who always scolds me, she's always eating at me,	
	At night she scolds me at least seven times	
	So severely, I think I shall die,	
	And if I defend myself when she hits me,	
	She does it even more. Then everything	80
	goes wrong and	
	She will not suffer flattery.	

Neighbor, this is only the chaff,
For every day, every hour
She makes my life sour.
This is an ordeal without end.
How shall I live in this pain?
How can any wife be so shrewish?
Neighbor, you know my ways.
I love to drink in the tavern.
But she loves to come here and scold me, 90
Kicking and screaming,
So I cannot refuse,
I must go home with her quickly.
Then she punches and hits me,
I think my ribs will crack.
I know she'd leave me alone,
If I'd take her drinking with me.
She'll pour one for herself
And drink it as if she were dying of thirst.
And she won't stop until she's drained 100
                                   the mug,
Even if she is bursting ...
If one mug is not enough,
She'll put the whole pot to her mouth.
She won't quit until she reaches the bottom.
Neighbor, her behavior dishonors me.
If I could find a way
That I could get peace,
That I could without shame shut her up,
Then I'd be master[6] all my days.
Maybe it would be good if I gave her 110
A fur pelt or some good cloth for a skirt.
Perhaps then she'd leave me in peace.
If I could just have peace for three days,
Then perhaps it would please her so much
That it would last six or seven months ...
Perhaps all our lives ... ?

	I could cajole her out of her shrewishness.	
NEIGHBOR:	Dear Jan, it bothers me	
	That you must have any discord.	
	I swear to you Jan, by St. Nick,	120
	We must endure sometimes before it's better	
	And sometimes keep still,	
	Even if we're in a bad way.	
	But really, your suffering bothers me.	
	They want to be flattered, some of these women,	
	Some are kept in their place with gifts,	
	There are some who need to be scolded,	
	And some who need to have their bodies beaten	
	With big sticks on their skin.	
	Still, they never come to good,	130
	And always remain shrewish.	
	It seems to me that the best advice is:	
	Bribe them with gifts, if you can,	
	Speak to them kindly all the time,	
	And then she might leave off her shrewishness.	
	It's a bad wife who won't settle down.	
	Neighbor, try this, it might work.	
JAN:	Gladly, Neighbor, without delay.	
	Adieu, Neighbor, I must go.	

[*Exit* NEIGHBOR, JAN *going to his house*]

	Now let us see how she will welcome me,	140
	When she sees me coming into the house.	
BETTE:	Look, our Lady damn him!	
	Here he comes, may God make him smart!	
	He makes me so miserable	
	With his drinking day and night!	
	I have a right to cry, "Oh woe is me!"	
	That I ever married such a man.	
	Now go, you bum, God give you shame!	
	Get some water and get it quick,	
	Or I will tread on	150

	Your skin under my feet. You will truly regret	
	That you ever saw me.	
	He is so drunk he can't stand	
	On his feet, the dirty bastard.	
	Get out of my sight, now!	
JAN:	Dear Bette, be at peace,	
	Truly, I haven't had anything to drink today.	
BETTE:	You'd lie even if they'd rip your limbs off,	
	Do you think I don't smell you?	
	You're twitching like a new-born chick.	160
	Go and do what I told you,	
	Or I'll give you such a whack	
	That it'll crack your ribs.	
JAN:	Dear Bette, now stop your talking.	
	If I could get your friendship,	
	By God, it would be for both our good.	
	If you would let me be the lord	
	Of our entire household	
	For three days, and then never again,	
	I would give you such a jewel, for which	170
	There is not a woman in these streets	
	Who would not let her husband	
	Be at peace for the entire year.	
	A good fur pelt, as your heart desires it,	
	I bought today from Peter.	
	He brought it for me from England.	
	This one will be yours, if you will let me	
	Be master for three days, everything just	
	as it should be.	
	Do you want it, now tell me?	
BETTE:	Fie on your pelt! Fie!	180
	You probably bought it for another tramp,	
	A tart, a nasty feeling that would give me!	
	Yup! That's who you bought it for!	
JAN:	Dear sweetheart, this is nonsense,	
	Take it and do it, this I counsel you.	

BETTE:	I will, for it might shame me
	If you gave it to a whore other than me.
	But I am right to say, "Fie,"
	If anyone knew that I sold myself thus.
	But let us make it a secret 190
	And do not tell anyone.
JAN:	Not I, on my word of honor,
	I shall be quiet, completely silent.
BETTE:	Then do all that you want
	And be master and lord for
	Three days and then nevermore.
	Still . . . it will seem longer to me. . . .

              [*Exit* BETTE]

JAN:	Wow! Now I am lord of all,
	Take my hat! Get scrubbing and scouring!
	Where are the bluffers, my neighbors, now? 200
	I think I'll go and have a drink.

          [JAN *leaving his house and on his way* . . .]

        If I see any, I'll give 'em a signal,
        For I want to go and drink beer.
        They're all sitting by their fires
        Spinning thread, the poor bastards.
        They don't dare go drinking because of
                                        their wives
        Who scold and badger them.
        My wife would rather break
        Both her legs than do that,
        For I would take her on,   210
        It would be an example to them all.
        Fie on those dopes! Fie on them! Fie!
        Those who let their wives keep them down!
        But truly, I know well, it's to no avail.[7]
        I want to go drink without worry and
        Even if I don't come home before morning
        My wife won't mind.

	She scours, she scrubs, she spins, she sews,	
	And does her duties in the house.	
	There she sits as quiet as a mouse	220
	And does the best she can.	
	I think no man ever saw a better wife	
	Now I want to go drinking, I want to get smashed.	
	[*Entering the tavern*]	
NEIGHBOR:	Master Neighbor, drinking? Tell me, listen!	
	Neighbor, how did it go?	
JAN:	I'll tell you all, I'll not spare a word,	
	But first I must have a drink.	
NEIGHBOR:	Take a mug, I'll pour for you.	
	Drink up, it's good beer.	
JAN:	Ah, me! God brought me here.	230
	This beer makes everything better.	
NEIGHBOR:	Neighbor, tell me now, what did your wife say?	
	For if I knew, it would give me great pleasure.	
JAN:	Neighbor, I'll tell you plainly,	
	For you are my best friend,	
	I got rid of my annoyance.	
	If you want to know how,	
	You must come and eat with me today,	
	I bid you come, you and your wife.	
	You shall hear, how with loving, I	240
	Have become the lord of the house, completely.	
	I can now go drinking when I want	
	Without being scolded by my wife.	
	I have been married for twenty years and five,	
	And in my heart I never had rest—	
	I bore it all, I put up with everything	
	Until this day.	
	And therefore I bid you	
	To come and eat with me	
	Right away and not to forget this,	250

Three Days Lord

	Because now I alone am
	Master of our house in every way.
	Come quickly without delay.
NEIGHBOR:	Go and set the table.
	I will come. I won't renege.
JAN:	I will go and set the table.
	Follow me right away and bring Betten.[8]
	[*Exit* JAN]
NEIGHBOR:	Gladly, Neighbor. And I won't renege.
	[NEIGHBOR *arriving at his own house*]
	Lijsbeth! Lijsbeth! you must come along.
	Jan, our neighbor, bids us
	To come and eat with him
	For he claims
	That never in his life
	Have things gone so well with his wife
	As now, this day today.
	But he has his peace
	For three days only, his respite
	May only last until vespers.
	Lijsbeth, you must make yourself ready.
WIFE:	Imberecht, if he invited me along too
	Then I want to go right away.
	I think that he won't keep
	His peace and quiet for very long.
	But he would not want to invite us
	If Bette were to get angry.
	Let's go, Imberecht, without lingering,
	This sounds really good to me.
NEIGHBOR:	Now let's go quickly without delay.
	They'll put us next to the fire.
	[JAN *and* BETTE's *house*]
JAN:	Bette, now give us a warm welcome!
	Is everything ready so we can eat?

BETTE: As you know, I think he will come,
Our neighbor and his wife.
Of course! Food here is scarce.
But you were smart to invite guests,
Because there is nothing more than this here.⁹
But I am content, let them come.
St. Mary! You quickly have figured out
How to be lord of the house!
Still, you might be put to shame   290
If you tried anything too excessive.
JAN: Bette, I have to leave off this argument
Because our neighbors are here.

[*Enter* NEIGHBOR *and his* WIFE]

NEIGHBOR: God and St. Michael,
May you have peace!
JAN: Welcome, neighbor, go and wash,
Sit there and your wife here,
And I will sit by the fire.
Bette, serve us salt and bread,
And all the food, great and small.   300
Get us wine and bring us cups,
From the inn called the "Tap,"¹⁰
That's the best in the town.
BETTE [*aside*]: I hope your mother drops dead!¹¹
You won't order me around like this for long.
NEIGHBOR: I never heard of a shrewish wife
Who was ever so sweetly disposed.
I see clearly that one will do a lot for money.
The one who can give and keep quiet,
Can do whatever he wants.   310
Yet still they say, "With nothing
Can a shrewish wife be tamed."
Dear neighbor, how can this be?
BETTE: Now drink up! Here is the wine.
NEIGHBOR: Welcome! Now give her to drink.

BETTE:	By God! you don't have to pour for me.	
	If you want anything else, just let me know,	
	So I can do it and also come and eat.	
	Now tell me and be finished.	
JAN:	Bette, this is just the chaff.	320
	You have to prepare a fruit tarte for us,	
	One we can eat before we part.	
	Now go and quickly put on the fire	
	And make no protest!	
	It must be as I tell you.	
BETTE:	I'd rather eat right now	
	Than to go do something else.	
JAN:	Now go and don't be so bold	
	To refrain from doing it, for I do not lie,	
	There will soon be more punches flying	330
	About your ears than pence to a pound.¹²	
BETTE:	I'd rather hunker down	
	And do the best I can.	
JAN:	Don't talk like a man!	
	It's an old saying:	
	"No ass is any good without control!"	
	Now eat and drink, my dear neighbors.	
	By God, she'll pay for that pelt,	
	The one I gave her	
	So I could live in peace	340
	And be the lord for three days.	
NEIGHBOR:	Jan, that's enough,	
	Nothing more today.	
BETTE:	Now taste. Does it please you well?	
	To me, it's pretty good.	
JAN:	It is not! It didn't turn out,	
	It's too thin. Do you want to teach me	
	How to make a proper fruit tarte?	
	Go and do it again,	
	For it seems to me that you've gone mad.	350
	A good tarte? What do you say about it?	

NEIGHBOR: I think I like it quite well.
I've got slobber up to my ears.
JAN: Yes, neighbor, you'll have to burp,[13]
And then, Bette, you shall drink,
Pour me on the double,
"Et tantos je buveray."[14]

[*Exit* BETTE]

NEIGHBOR: Neighbor, now you're happy.
Still you're nothing but a rotten Walloon.[15]
JAN: Doesn't it seem to you from what I say   360
That now I am able to control my wife?
I'll make her jump through a hoop,
Before you part from here.

[*The women aside and alone*]

WIFE: My friend, how did this happen?
Why did you sell yourself like this?
"Seek and you shall find it."
That's what your husband's doing now,
                    it seems to me.
He didn't know how to be your master
But for this cunning trick.
If he remains the master now   370
We shall suffer pain for it, we shall smart.
Friend, I swear you by St. Nick's heart,
Before I would make a deal over a pelt,
I'd rather hit him so hard
That he spat blood, the dirty bastard.
You should think, unhappy woman,
If you need a pelt or a skirt,
Then speak a few sweet words to him,
And you shall have what you desire.
Then right away change your tone   380
And you'll be mistress just like before.
He'll always want to be the boss, for
All men want to control their wives this way.

	He can go ahead with his business, but	
	There is no woman in the streets[16]	
	Who is not made worse by what you've done.	
BETTE:	Dear friend, now keep quiet,	
	By St. Nick's agony, I'll do as you say!	
	I'd rather hang in a basket	
	In the smoke of our chimney....	390
	Fie! God damn that fur pelt,	
	That I ever gave myself over to him.[17]	

[*Enter* JAN]

JAN:	My wife is really hustling now.	
	I will teach her how to make a fruit tarte.	
	We'll see who pulls the longest straw.[18]	
	I've never seen a bigger fool.	
NEIGHBOR:	Dear Jan, believe me,	
	Here is food better than food,	
	This I will teach you also, Lise,	
	To run and hustle during the meal.	400
WIFE:	By God, with that you wouldn't win much.	
	And neither will he, that I know well.	
JAN:	I want her to be quick	
	To do what I have requested of her....	

Notes

1. His name, "Ghebeur," means the equivalent of "neighbor"; Jan is later (v. 72) also referred to by this Ghebeur as "ghebeur," or neighbor.
2. The implication being, you too may have a shrewish wife at home.
3. A measure, more for dry goods, used here to be funny.
4. "Coels sette," St. Nicolaas' ass, also sometimes by God's ass, or, Mohamed's ass.
5. It is unclear here to whom "the wife" is speaking since Ghebuer goes right on with his monologue as if no one else is there.
6. As in the title, a gentleman, a lord.
7. He finds no one to go drinking with, so he might as well go alone.
8. Jan is referring to Neighbor's wife, Lijsbeth, whose nickname, "Betten," is very similar to Jan's wife's name, "Bette," suggesting the interchangibilty of these women, both potential and collusive "shrews." See Lijsbeth's advice to Bette, for example, v. 364–86.
9. Bette is being ironic, there's nothing to eat in the house.
10. The "tap" may refer to a pub called the Tap, as I indicate, or it may just mean a bar, a place to serve beer from. See Leendertz, v. 2, 525.
11. This is a curse which is literally, "I hope your mother's got a migraine," in the sense of "I hope your mother's ears are burning," meaning "I hope your mother pays for having given birth to you."
12. "Ouder grote" were old "grotes" worth half a nickle, a shilling.
13. A line which is unclear, because "booren" has so many possible variants. I have suggested a logical (given the context of eating too much) and humorous translation. Others have suggested that "booren" is really a variation of "gebeuren" meaning it will happen. In other words, Jan is saying "things like [getting all slobbered up] can happen." Another variation, according to Leendertz, goes something like: "that won't work." See Leendertz, v. 2, 525–6 and Stellinga, *Drie*, 27.
14. "And at the same time, I'll drink."
15. A curse, "Wale," the Dutch "Waal," or walloon, and "verrot," rotten or dirty. Neighbor here is commenting on Jan's French.
16. That is, "the world."
17. That I ever let him have control over me.
18. Who will win this, who is really the boss.

Carleton Renaissance Plays in Translation

This volume of the Renaissance Plays was produced using the TeX typesetting system, with Adobe Palatino PostScript fonts and in-house critical edition macros.

PRINTED AND BOUND
IN BOUCHERVILLE, QUÉBEC, CANADA
BY MARC VEILLEUX IMPRIMEUR INC.
IN FEBRUARY, 1997